MUSHROOMS

OF THE

SOUTHEAST

IDENTIFICATION
RECORD BOOK

Hello Wild

Your Feedback is Appreciated!!!

Please consider leaving us "5 Stars" on your Amazon review.

Thank you!

MUSHROOMS OF THE SOUTHEAST

This Mushrooom Identification Record Book
Belongs To:

_____

There are thousands of species of mushrooms in the Southeast. The region consists of states Missouri, Arkansas, Louisiana, Kentucky, West Virginia, Virginia, Tennessee, North Carolina, South Carolina, Mississippi, Alabama, Georgia, and Florida. With a climate that is generally described as humid usually with highs in the 80's and 90's, a wide variety of mushrooms grow and thrive in the landscape. While many types are highly toxic, there are a number of edible mushrooms as well. Do not eat any mushroom without checking in person with a local, live mushroom collector/expert.

Use this record book to identify and record the many types of mushrooms you come across!

Location

Site / GPS: _____ Date: _____

◯ Living Tree ◯ Leaf Litter ◯ Mulch ◯ Dead Tree or Wood ◯ Grass
◯ Soil ◯ Other _____

Type of Tree(s) On or Near: _____

Forest Type: ◯ Deciduous ◯ Coniferous ◯ Tropical ◯ Other _____

Weather Conditions: _____

General

Size (overall height): _____ Color: _____ Spore Color: _____

Texture: ◯ Tough ◯ Brittle ◯ Leathery ◯ Woody ◯ Soft ◯ Slimy
◯ Spongy ◯ Powdery ◯ Waxy ◯ Rubbery ◯ Watery (Other) _____

Bruising When Touched? ◯ Yes ◯ No   Notes: _____

Structures: ◯ Cup ◯ Ring ◯ Warts   _____

Cap Characteristics

Campanulate
(bell-shaped)

Conical
(triangular)

Cylindrical
(shaped like half an egg)

Convex
(outwardly rounded)

Flat
(with top of uniform height)

Infundibuliform
(deeply, depressed, funnel-shaped)

Depressed
(with a low central region)

Umbonate
(with a central bump or knob)

Surface Markings (warts, scales, slime, etc.): _____

Cap Margin: Smooth, Inrolled, Sinuous/Wavy, Other:_____

Color Changes: _____

Undercap

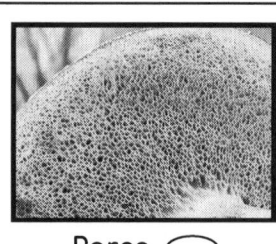

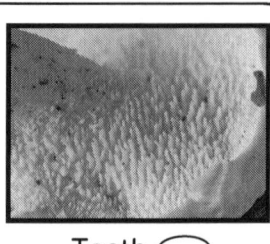

Gills ◯

Attachment: Free or Decurrent

Spacing: Crowded, Close, Distant, Subdistant

Color/Bruising: _____

Pores ◯

Color: _____

Pore Size: _____

Pore Pattern: _____

Teeth ◯

Color: _____

Teeth Length: _____

Flesh: Soft or Tough

○ Free
(gills not attached to stem)

Adnexed
(gills attached narrowly to stem)

Sinuate
(gills smoothly notched and running briefly down stem)

Adnate
(gills widely attached widely to stem)

Descending
(gills running down stem for some length)

Tapering

Equal

Club-Shaped

Bulbous

Cup (volva)

Morels
- Edible ☺
- Honeycombed cap
- Most morels cap is longer than stem
- Spore print is usually light colored
- Interior is hollow

Puffballs
- Edible ☺
- Color is white
- Rounded-shaped balls with or without spiny warts on top
- Can be mistaken for golf ball, baseball or even soccer ball

Fly Agaric
- Poisonous ☻
- Red-brown cap - irregularly lobed, like a brain
- Tube-like hollows
- Yellowish spore print
- Smooth with more wrinkles as it ages

Oyster Mushroom
- Edible ☺
- Grows on hardwood trees
- Gills descend to base
- Gills are not saw toothed or ruffled
- Spore deposit gray

Death Cap
- Poisonous ☻
- Flattened top
- White cap with brownish scales
- Gills are free and white, turning green as they mature

Jack O'Lantern
- Poisonous ☻
- Bright orange to yellowish
- Grows in clusters
- Cap convex
- Gills narrow
- Cream spore print

Lion's Mane
- Edible ☺
- Covered all over with long, spine-like hairs
- Club-shaped fruit bodies
- Common on hardwoods

Destroying Angel
- Poisonous ☻
- White stalk and gills
- White cap or white edge and yellowish, pinkish, or tan center
- Egg-shaped cap

Chicken of the Woods
- Edible ☺
- Fan-shaped and suede-like texture
- Fruitbody with yellow, round pores
- Brownish color

Chanterelle
- Edible ☺
- Shape looks like bell of a trumpet
- Bright yellow/orange
- Similar look to Jack o'Lantern

Deadly Galerina
- Poisonous ☻
- Brownish, sticky cap, yellowish to rusty gills, ring on stalk
- Edges are curved against gills
- Gills narrow, crowded

Witches' Butter
- Edible ☺
- Small, yellow, irregularly lobed, gelatinous masses
- Grows on dead deciduous wood, especially oaks

Spore Print

_____
_____
_____
_____
_____

Location

Site / GPS: _____ Date: _____

○ Living Tree ○ Leaf Litter ○ Mulch ○ Dead Tree or Wood ○ Grass
○ Soil ○ Other _____

Type of Tree(s) On or Near: _____

Forest Type: ○ Deciduous ○ Coniferous ○ Tropical ○ Other _____

Weather Conditions: _____

General

Size (overall height): _____ Color: _____ Spore Color: _____

Texture: ○ Tough ○ Brittle ○ Leathery ○ Woody ○ Soft ○ Slimy
○ Spongy ○ Powdery ○ Waxy ○ Rubbery ○ Watery (Other) _____

Bruising When Touched? ○ Yes ○ No   Notes: _____

Structures: ○ Cup ○ Ring ○ Warts   _____

Cap Characteristics

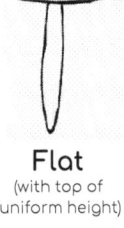

Campanulate
(bell-shaped)

Conical
(triangular)

Cylindrical
(shaped like half an egg)

Convex
(outwardly rounded)

Flat
(with top of
uniform height)

Infundibuliform
(deeply, depressed,
funnel-shaped)

Depressed
(with a low
central region)

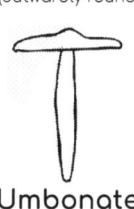

Umbonate
(with a central
bump or knob)

Surface Markings (warts, scales, slime, etc.): _____

Cap Margin: Smooth, Inrolled, Sinuous/Wavy, Other:_____

Color Changes: _____

Undercap

Gills ○

Attachment: Free or Decurrent

Spacing: Crowded, Close,
          Distant, Subdistant

Color/Bruising: _____

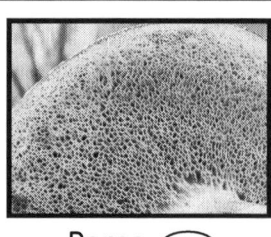

Pores ○

Color: _____

Pore Size: _____

Pore Pattern: _____

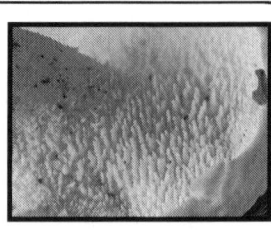

Teeth ○

Color: _____

Teeth Length: _____

Flesh: Soft or Tough

○ Free
(gills not attached to stem)

○ Adnexed
(gills attached narrowly to stem)

○ Sinuate
(gills smoothly notched and running briefly down stem)

○ Adnate
(gills widely attached widely to stem)

○ Descending
(gills running down stem for some length)

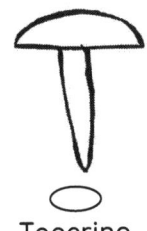  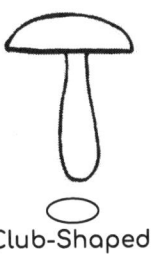 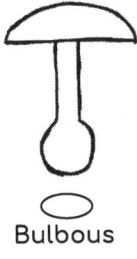 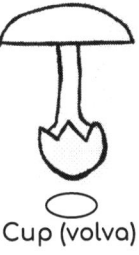 

○ Tapering

○ Equal

○ Club-Shaped

○ Bulbous

○ Cup (volva)

Morels

- Edible ☺
- Honeycombed cap
- Most morels cap is longer than stem
- Spore print is usually light colored
- Interior is hollow

Puffballs

- Edible ☺
- Color is white
- Rounded-shaped balls with or without spiny warts on top
- Can be mistaken for golf ball, baseball or even soccer ball

Fly Agaric

- Poisonous ☹
- Red-brown cap - irregularly lobed, like a brain
- Tube-like hollows
- Yellowish spore print
- Smooth with more wrinkles as it ages

Oyster Mushroom

- Edible ☺
- Grows on hardwood trees
- Gills descend to base
- Gills are not saw toothed or ruffled
- Spore deposit gray

Death Cap

- Poisonous ☹
- Flattened top
- White cap with brownish scales
- Gills are free and white, turning green as they mature

Jack O'Lantern

- Poisonous ☹
- Bright orange to yellowish
- Grows in clusters
- Cap convex
- Gills narrow
- Cream spore print

Lion's Mane

- Edible ☺
- Covered all over with long, spine-like hairs
- Club-shaped fruit bodies
- Common on hardwoods

Destroying Angel

- Poisonous ☹
- White stalk and gills
- White cap or white edge and yellowish, pinkish, or tan center
- Egg-shaped cap

Chicken of the Woods

- Edible ☺
- Fan-shaped and suede-like texture
- Fruitbody with yellow, round pores
- Brownish color

Chanterelle

- Edible ☺
- Shape looks like bell of a trumpet
- Bright yellow/orange
- Similar look to Jack o'Lantern

Deadly Galerina

- Poisonous ☹
- Brownish, sticky cap, yellowish to rusty gills, ring on stalk
- Edges are curved against gills
- Gills narrow, crowded

Witches' Butter

- Edible ☺
- Small, yellow, irregularly lobed, gelatinous masses
- Grows on dead deciduous wood, especially oaks

Spore Print

_____

_____

_____

_____

_____

_____

Location

Site / GPS: _____ Date: _____

○ Living Tree   ○ Leaf Litter   ○ Mulch   ○ Dead Tree or Wood   ○ Grass
○ Soil   ○ Other _____

Type of Tree(s) On or Near: _____

Forest Type: ○ Deciduous   ○ Coniferous   ○ Tropical   ○ Other _____

Weather Conditions: _____

General

Size (overall height): _____   Color: _____   Spore Color: _____

Texture: ○ Tough   ○ Brittle   ○ Leathery   ○ Woody   ○ Soft   ○ Slimy
○ Spongy   ○ Powdery   ○ Waxy   ○ Rubbery   ○ Watery   (Other) _____

Bruising When Touched?   ○ Yes   ○ No   Notes: _____

Structures: ○ Cup   ○ Ring   ○ Warts   _____

Cap Characteristics

Campanulate
(bell-shaped)

Conical
(triangular)

Cylindrical
(shaped like half an egg)

Convex
(outwardly rounded)

Flat
(with top of uniform height)

Infundibuliform
(deeply, depressed, funnel-shaped)

Depressed
(with a low central region)

Umbonate
(with a central bump or knob)

Surface Markings (warts, scales, slime, etc.): _____

Cap Margin: Smooth, Inrolled, Sinuous/Wavy, Other: _____

Color Changes: _____

Undercap

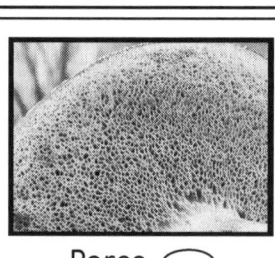

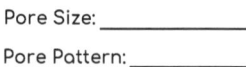

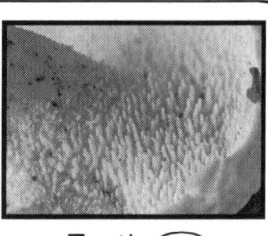

Gills ○
Attachment: Free or Decurrent

Spacing: Crowded, Close,
               Distant, Subdistant

Color/Bruising: _____

Pores ○
Color: _____

Pore Size: _____

Pore Pattern: _____

Teeth ○
Color: _____

Teeth Length: _____

Flesh: Soft or Tough

Free	Adnexed	Sinuate	Adnate	Descending
(gills not attached to stem)	(gills attached narrowly to stem)	(gills smoothly notched and running briefly down stem)	(gills widely attached widely to stem)	(gills running down stem for some length)

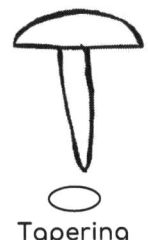  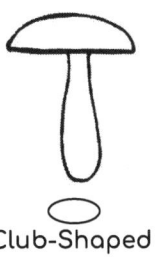 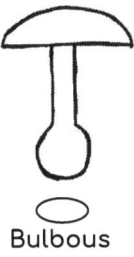  

Tapering	Equal	Club-Shaped	Bulbous	Cup (volva)

Morels
- Edible ☺
- Honeycombed cap
- Most morels cap is longer than stem
- Spore print is usually light colored
- Interior is hollow

Puffballs
- Edible ☺
- Color is white
- Rounded-shaped balls with or without spiny warts on top
- Can be mistaken for golf ball, baseball or even soccer ball

Fly Agaric
- Poisonous ☹
- Red-brown cap - irregularly lobed, like a brain
- Tube-like hollows
- Yellowish spore print
- Smooth with more wrinkles as it ages

Oyster Mushroom
- Edible ☺
- Grows on hardwood trees
- Gills descend to base
- Gills are not saw toothed or ruffled
- Spore deposit gray

Death Cap
- Poisonous ☹
- Flattened top
- White cap with brownish scales
- Gills are free and white, turning green as they mature

Jack O'Lantern
- Poisonous ☹
- Bright orange to yellowish
- Grows in clusters
- Cap convex
- Gills narrow
- Cream spore print

Lion's Mane
- Edible ☺
- Covered all over with long, spine-like hairs
- Club-shaped fruit bodies
- Common on hardwoods

Destroying Angel
- Poisonous ☹
- White stalk and gills
- White cap or white edge and yellowish, pinkish, or tan center
- Egg-shaped cap

Chicken of the Woods
- Edible ☺
- Fan-shaped and suede-like texture
- Fruitbody with yellow, round pores
- Brownish color

Chanterelle
- Edible ☺
- Shape looks like bell of a trumpet
- Bright yellow/orange
- Similar look to Jack o'Lantern

Deadly Galerina
- Poisonous ☹
- Brownish, sticky cap, yellowish to rusty gills, ring on stalk
- Edges are curved against gills
- Gills narrow, crowded

Witches' Butter
- Edible ☺
- Small, yellow, irregularly lobed, gelatinous masses
- Grows on dead deciduous wood, especially oaks

Spore Print

_____
_____
_____
_____
_____
_____

Location

Site / GPS: _____ Date: _____

○ Living Tree   ○ Leaf Litter   ○ Mulch   ○ Dead Tree or Wood   ○ Grass
○ Soil   ○ Other _____

Type of Tree(s) On or Near: _____

Forest Type: ○ Deciduous   ○ Coniferous   ○ Tropical   ○ Other _____

Weather Conditions: _____

General

Size (overall height): _____   Color: _____   Spore Color: _____

Texture: ○ Tough   ○ Brittle   ○ Leathery   ○ Woody   ○ Soft   ○ Slimy
○ Spongy   ○ Powdery   ○ Waxy   ○ Rubbery   ○ Watery   (Other) _____

Bruising When Touched? ○ Yes   ○ No   Notes: _____

Structures: ○ Cup   ○ Ring   ○ Warts   _____

Cap Characteristics

Campanulate
(bell-shaped)

Conical
(triangular)

Cylindrical
(shaped like half an egg)

Convex
(outwardly rounded)

Flat
(with top of
uniform height)

Infundibuliform
(deeply, depressed,
funnel-shaped)

Depressed
(with a low
central region)

Umbonate
(with a central
bump or knob)

Surface Markings (warts, scales, slime, etc.): _____

Cap Margin: Smooth, Inrolled, Sinuous/Wavy, Other: _____

Color Changes: _____

Undercap

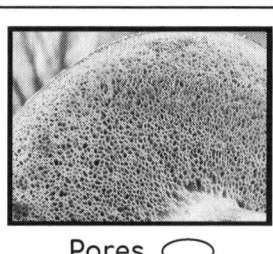

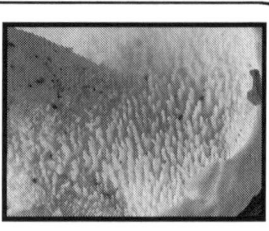

Gills ○

Attachment: Free or Decurrent

Spacing: Crowded, Close,
Distant, Subdistant

Color/Bruising: _____

Pores ○

Color: _____

Pore Size: _____

Pore Pattern: _____

Teeth ○

Color: _____

Teeth Length: _____

Flesh: Soft or Tough

 **Free**
(gills not attached to stem)

 **Adnexed**
(gills attached narrowly to stem)

 **Sinuate**
(gills smoothly notched and running briefly down stem)

Adnate
(gills widely attached widely to stem)

Descending
(gills running down stem for some length)

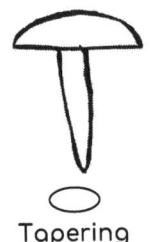

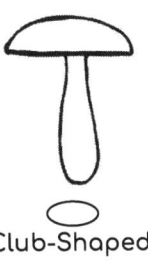
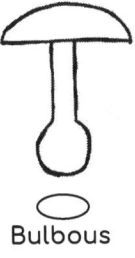

Tapering **Equal** **Club-Shaped** **Bulbous** **Cup (volva)**

Morels
- Edible ☺
- Honeycombed cap
- Most morels cap is longer than stem
- Spore print is usually light colored
- Interior is hollow

Puffballs
- Edible ☺
- Color is white
- Rounded-shaped balls with or without spiny warts on top
- Can be mistaken for golf ball, baseball or even soccer ball

Fly Agaric
- Poisonous ☹
- Red-brown cap - irregularly lobed, like a brain
- Tube-like hollows
- Yellowish spore print
- Smooth with more wrinkles as it ages

Oyster Mushroom
- Edible ☺
- Grows on hardwood trees
- Gills descend to base
- Gills are not saw toothed or ruffled
- Spore deposit gray

Death Cap
- Poisonous ☹
- Flattened top
- White cap with brownish scales
- Gills are free and white, turning green as they mature

Jack O'Lantern
- Poisonous ☹
- Bright orange to yellowish
- Grows in clusters
- Cap convex
- Gills narrow
- Cream spore print

Lion's Mane
- Edible ☺
- Covered all over with long, spine-like hairs
- Club-shaped fruit bodies
- Common on hardwoods

Destroying Angel
- Poisonous ☹
- White stalk and gills
- White cap or white edge and yellowish, pinkish, or tan center
- Egg-shaped cap

Chicken of the Woods
- Edible ☺
- Fan-shaped and suede-like texture
- Fruitbody with yellow, round pores
- Brownish color

Chanterelle
- Edible ☺
- Shape looks like bell of a trumpet
- Bright yellow/orange
- Similar look to Jack o'Lantern

Deadly Galerina
- Poisonous ☹
- Brownish, sticky cap, yellowish to rusty gills, ring on stalk
- Edges are curved against gills
- Gills narrow, crowded

Witches' Butter
- Edible ☺
- Small, yellow, irregularly lobed, gelatinous masses
- Grows on dead deciduous wood, especially oaks

Spore Print

_____

_____

_____

_____

_____

_____

_____

Location

Site / GPS: _____ Date: _____

○ Living Tree ○ Leaf Litter ○ Mulch ○ Dead Tree or Wood ○ Grass
○ Soil ○ Other _____

Type of Tree(s) On or Near: _____

Forest Type: ○ Deciduous ○ Coniferous ○ Tropical ○ Other _____

Weather Conditions: _____

General

Size (overall height): _____ Color: _____ Spore Color: _____

Texture: ○ Tough ○ Brittle ○ Leathery ○ Woody ○ Soft ○ Slimy
○ Spongy ○ Powdery ○ Waxy ○ Rubbery ○ Watery (Other) _____

Bruising When Touched? ○ Yes ○ No   Notes: _____

Structures: ○ Cup ○ Ring ○ Warts   _____

Cap Characteristics

Campanulate
(bell-shaped)

Conical
(triangular)

Cylindrical
(shaped like half an egg)

Convex
(outwardly rounded)

Flat
(with top of
uniform height)

Infundibuliform
(deeply, depressed,
funnel-shaped)

Depressed
(with a low
central region)

Umbonate
(with a central
bump or knob)

Surface Markings (warts, scales, slime, etc.): _____

Cap Margin: Smooth, Inrolled, Sinuous/Wavy, Other: _____

Color Changes: _____

Undercap

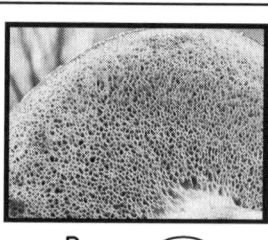

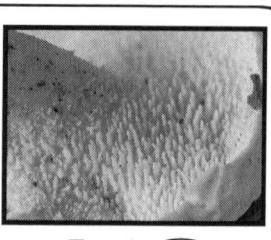

Gills ○

Attachment: Free or Decurrent

Spacing: Crowded, Close,
Distant, Subdistant

Color/Bruising: _____

Pores ○

Color: _____

Pore Size: _____

Pore Pattern: _____

Teeth ○

Color: _____

Teeth Length: _____

Flesh: Soft or Tough

◯ **Free**
(gills not attached to stem)

◯ **Adnexed**
(gills attached narrowly to stem)

◯ **Sinuate**
(gills smoothly notched and running briefly down stem)

◯ **Adnate**
(gills widely attached widely to stem)

◯ **Descenting**
(gills running down stem for some length)

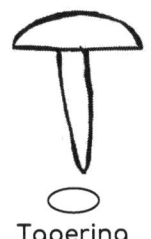  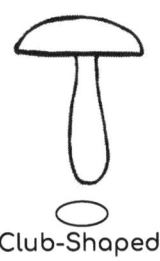 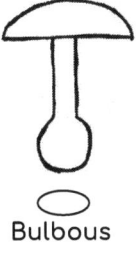 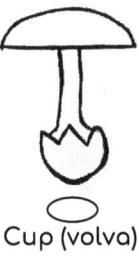 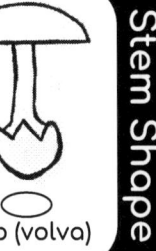

◯ **Tapering**   ◯ **Equal**   ◯ **Club-Shaped**   ◯ **Bulbous**   ◯ **Cup (volva)**

Morels
- Edible ☺
- Honeycombed cap
- Most morels cap is longer than stem
- Spore print is usually light colored
- Interior is hollow

Puffballs
- Edible ☺
- Color is white
- Rounded-shaped balls with or without spiny warts on top
- Can be mistaken for golf ball, baseball or even soccer ball

Fly Agaric
- Poisonous ☹
- Red-brown cap - irregularly lobed, like a brain
- Tube-like hollows
- Yellowish spore print
- Smooth with more wrinkles as it ages

Oyster Mushroom
- Edible ☺
- Grows on hardwood trees
- Gills descend to base
- Gills are not saw toothed or ruffled
- Spore deposit gray

Death Cap
- Poisonous ☹
- Flattened top
- White cap with brownish scales
- Gills are free and white, turning green as they mature

Jack O'Lantern
- Poisonous ☹
- Bright orange to yellowish
- Grows in clusters
- Cap convex
- Gills narrow
- Cream spore print

Lion's Mane
- Edible ☺
- Covered all over with long, spine-like hairs
- Club-shaped fruit bodies
- Common on hardwoods

Destroying Angel
- Poisonous ☹
- White stalk and gills
- White cap or white edge and yellowish, pinkish, or tan center
- Egg-shaped cap

Chicken of the Woods
- Edible ☺
- Fan-shaped and suede-like texture
- Fruitbody with yellow, round pores
- Brownish color

Chanterelle
- Edible ☺
- Shape looks like bell of a trumpet
- Bright yellow/orange
- Similar look to Jack o'Lantern

Deadly Galerina
- Poisonous ☹
- Brownish, sticky cap, yellowish to rusty gills, ring on stalk
- Edges are curved against gills
- Gills narrow, crowded

Witches' Butter
- Edible ☺
- Small, yellow, irregularly lobed, gelatinous masses
- Grows on dead deciduous wood, especially oaks

Spore Print

Location

Site / GPS: _____ Date: _____

◯ Living Tree ◯ Leaf Litter ◯ Mulch ◯ Dead Tree or Wood ◯ Grass
◯ Soil ◯ Other _____

Type of Tree(s) On or Near: _____

Forest Type: ◯ Deciduous ◯ Coniferous ◯ Tropical ◯ Other _____

Weather Conditions: _____

General

Size (overall height): _____ Color: _____ Spore Color: _____

Texture: ◯ Tough ◯ Brittle ◯ Leathery ◯ Woody ◯ Soft ◯ Slimy
◯ Spongy ◯ Powdery ◯ Waxy ◯ Rubbery ◯ Watery (Other) _____

Bruising When Touched? ◯ Yes ◯ No   Notes: _____

Structures: ◯ Cup ◯ Ring ◯ Warts   _____

Cap Characteristics

Campanulate
(bell-shaped)

Conical
(triangular)

Cylindrical
(shaped like half an egg)

Convex
(outwardly rounded)

Flat
(with top of
uniform height)

Infundibuliform
(deeply, depressed,
funnel-shaped)

Depressed
(with a low
central region)

Umbonate
(with a central
bump or knob)

Surface Markings (warts, scales, slime, etc.): _____

Cap Margin: Smooth, Inrolled, Sinuous/Wavy, Other:_____

Color Changes: _____

Undercap

Gills ◯

Attachment: Free or Decurrent

Spacing: Crowded, Close,
Distant, Subdistant

Color/Bruising: _____

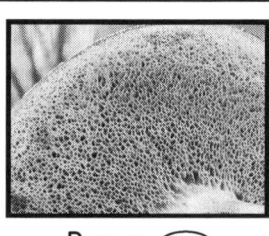

Pores ◯

Color: _____

Pore Size: _____

Pore Pattern: _____

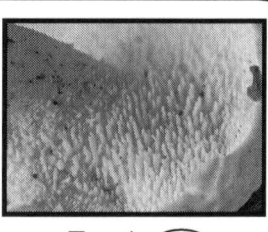

Teeth ◯

Color: _____

Teeth Length: _____

Flesh: Soft or Tough

○ Free
(gills not attached to stem)

○ Adnexed
(gills attached narrowly to stem)

○ Sinuate
(gills smoothly notched and running briefly down stem)

○ Adnate
(gills widely attached widely to stem)

○ Descending
(gills running down stem for some length)

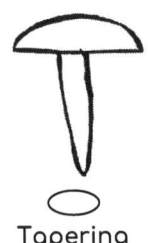  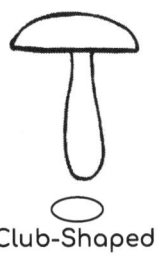 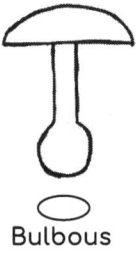 

○ Tapering

○ Equal

○ Club-Shaped

○ Bulbous

○ Cup (volva)

Morels
- Edible ☺
- Honeycombed cap
- Most morels cap is longer than stem
- Spore print is usually light colored
- Interior is hollow

Puffballs
- Edible ☺
- Color is white
- Rounded-shaped balls with or without spiny warts on top
- Can be mistaken for golf ball, baseball or even soccer ball

Fly Agaric
- Poisonous ☹
- Red-brown cap - irregularly lobed, like a brain
- Tube-like hollows
- Yellowish spore print
- Smooth with more wrinkles as it ages

Oyster Mushroom
- Edible ☺
- Grows on hardwood trees
- Gills descend to base
- Gills are not saw toothed or ruffled
- Spore deposit gray

Death Cap
- Poisonous ☹
- Flattened top
- White cap with brownish scales
- Gills are free and white, turning green as they mature

Jack O'Lantern
- Poisonous ☹
- Bright orange to yellowish
- Grows in clusters
- Cap convex
- Gills narrow
- Cream spore print

Lion's Mane
- Edible ☺
- Covered all over with long, spine-like hairs
- Club-shaped fruit bodies
- Common on hardwoods

Destroying Angel
- Poisonous ☹
- White stalk and gills
- White cap or white edge and yellowish, pinkish, or tan center
- Egg-shaped cap

Chicken of the Woods
- Edible ☺
- Fan-shaped and suede-like texture
- Fruitbody with yellow, round pores
- Brownish color

Chanterelle
- Edible ☺
- Shape looks like bell of a trumpet
- Bright yellow/orange
- Similar look to Jack o'Lantern

Deadly Galerina
- Poisonous ☹
- Brownish, sticky cap, yellowish to rusty gills, ring on stalk
- Edges are curved against gills
- Gills narrow, crowded

Witches' Butter
- Edible ☺
- Small, yellow, irregularly lobed, gelatinous masses
- Grows on dead deciduous wood, especially oaks

Spore Print

_____

_____

_____

_____

_____

_____

Location

Site / GPS: _____ Date: _____

○ Living Tree   ○ Leaf Litter   ○ Mulch   ○ Dead Tree or Wood   ○ Grass
○ Soil   ○ Other _____

Type of Tree(s) On or Near: _____

Forest Type: ○ Deciduous   ○ Coniferous   ○ Tropical   ○ Other _____

Weather Conditions: _____

General

Size (overall height): _____   Color: _____   Spore Color: _____

Texture: ○ Tough   ○ Brittle   ○ Leathery   ○ Woody   ○ Soft   ○ Slimy
○ Spongy   ○ Powdery   ○ Waxy   ○ Rubbery   ○ Watery   (Other) _____

Bruising When Touched? ○ Yes   ○ No   Notes: _____

Structures: ○ Cup   ○ Ring   ○ Warts   _____

Cap Characteristics

Campanulate
(bell-shaped)

Conical
(triangular)

Cylindrical
(shaped like half an egg)

Convex
(outwardly rounded)

Flat
(with top of
uniform height)

Infundibuliform
(deeply, depressed,
funnel-shaped)

Depressed
(with a low
central region)

Umbonate
(with a central
bump or knob)

Surface Markings (warts, scales, slime, etc.): _____

Cap Margin: Smooth, Inrolled, Sinuous/Wavy, Other: _____

Color Changes: _____

Undercap

Gills ○

Attachment: Free or Decurrent

Spacing: Crowded, Close,
            Distant, Subdistant

Color/Bruising: _____

Pores ○

Color: _____

Pore Size: _____

Pore Pattern: _____

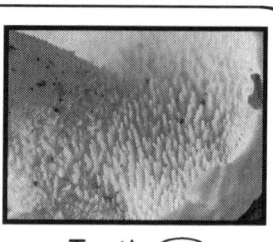

Teeth ○

Color: _____

Teeth Length: _____

Flesh: Soft or Tough

Free	Adnexed	Sinuate	Adnate	Descending
(gills not attached to stem)	(gills attached narrowly to stem)	(gills smoothly notched and running briefly down stem)	(gills widely attached widely to stem)	(gills running down stem for some length)

Tapering	Equal	Club-Shaped	Bulbous	Cup (volva)

Morels

- Edible ☺
- Honeycombed cap
- Most morels cap is longer than stem
- Spore print is usually light colored
- Interior is hollow

Puffballs

- Edible ☺
- Color is white
- Rounded-shaped balls with or without spiny warts on top
- Can be mistaken for golf ball, baseball or even soccer ball

Fly Agaric

- Poisonous ☹
- Red-brown cap - irregularly lobed, like a brain
- Tube-like hollows
- Yellowish spore print
- Smooth with more wrinkles as it ages

Oyster Mushroom

- Edible ☺
- Grows on hardwood trees
- Gills descend to base
- Gills are not saw toothed or ruffled
- Spore deposit gray

Death Cap

- Poisonous ☹
- Flattened top
- White cap with brownish scales
- Gills are free and white, turning green as they mature

Jack O'Lantern

- Poisonous ☹
- Bright orange to yellowish
- Grows in clusters
- Cap convex
- Gills narrow
- Cream spore print

Lion's Mane

- Edible ☺
- Covered all over with long, spine-like hairs
- Club-shaped fruit bodies
- Common on hardwoods

Destroying Angel

- Poisonous ☹
- White stalk and gills
- White cap or white edge and yellowish, pinkish, or tan center
- Egg-shaped cap

Chicken of the Woods

- Edible ☺
- Fan-shaped and suede-like texture
- Fruitbody with yellow, round pores
- Brownish color

Chanterelle

- Edible ☺
- Shape looks like bell of a trumpet
- Bright yellow/orange
- Similar look to Jack o'Lantern

Deadly Galerina

- Poisonous ☹
- Brownish, sticky cap, yellowish to rusty gills, ring on stalk
- Edges are curved against gills
- Gills narrow, crowded

Witches' Butter

- Edible ☺
- Small, yellow, irregularly lobed, gelatinous masses
- Grows on dead deciduous wood, especially oaks

Spore Print

Location

Site / GPS: _____ Date: _____

○ Living Tree   ○ Leaf Litter   ○ Mulch   ○ Dead Tree or Wood   ○ Grass
○ Soil   ○ Other _____

Type of Tree(s) On or Near: _____

Forest Type: ○ Deciduous   ○ Coniferous   ○ Tropical   ○ Other _____

Weather Conditions: _____

General

Size (overall height): _____   Color: _____   Spore Color: _____

Texture: ○ Tough   ○ Brittle   ○ Leathery   ○ Woody   ○ Soft   ○ Slimy
○ Spongy   ○ Powdery   ○ Waxy   ○ Rubbery   ○ Watery   (Other) _____

Bruising When Touched? ○ Yes   ○ No   Notes: _____

Structures: ○ Cup   ○ Ring   ○ Warts   _____

Cap Characteristics

Campanulate
(bell-shaped)

Conical
(triangular)

Cylindrical
(shaped like half an egg)

Convex
(outwardly rounded)

Flat
(with top of
uniform height)

Infundibuliform
(deeply, depressed,
funnel-shaped)

Depressed
(with a low
central region)

Umbonate
(with a central
bump or knob)

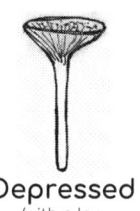
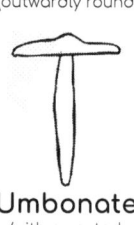

Surface Markings (warts, scales, slime, etc.): _____

Cap Margin: Smooth, Inrolled, Sinuous/Wavy, Other: _____

Color Changes: _____

Undercap

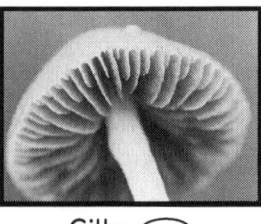
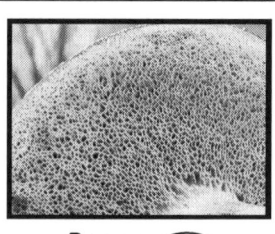
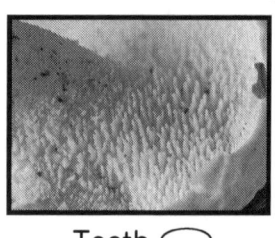

Gills ○

Attachment: Free or Decurrent

Spacing: Crowded, Close,
          Distant, Subdistant

Color/Bruising: _____

Pores ○

Color: _____

Pore Size: _____

Pore Pattern: _____

Teeth ○

Color: _____

Teeth Length: _____

Flesh: Soft or Tough

Free	Adnexed	Sinuate	Adnate	Descending
(gills not attached to stem)	(gills attached narrowly to stem)	(gills smoothly notched and running briefly down stem)	(gills widely attached widely to stem)	(gills running down stem for some length)

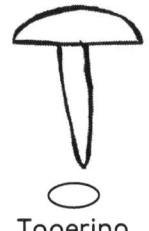  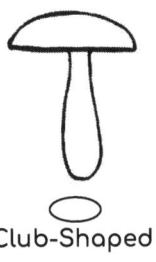 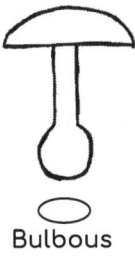 

Tapering   Equal   Club-Shaped   Bulbous   Cup (volva)

Morels
- Edible ☺
- Honeycombed cap
- Most morels cap is longer than stem
- Spore print is usually light colored
- Interior is hollow

Puffballs
- Edible ☺
- Color is white
- Rounded-shaped balls with or without spiny warts on top
- Can be mistaken for golf ball, baseball or even soccer ball

Fly Agaric
- Poisonous ☹
- Red-brown cap - irregularly lobed, like a brain
- Tube-like hollows
- Yellowish spore print
- Smooth with more wrinkles as it ages

Oyster Mushroom
- Edible ☺
- Grows on hardwood trees
- Gills descend to base
- Gills are not saw toothed or ruffled
- Spore deposit gray

Death Cap
- Poisonous ☹
- Flattened top
- White cap with brownish scales
- Gills are free and white, turning green as they mature

Jack O'Lantern
- Poisonous ☹
- Bright orange to yellowish
- Grows in clusters
- Cap convex
- Gills narrow
- Cream spore print

Lion's Mane
- Edible ☺
- Covered all over with long, spine-like hairs
- Club-shaped fruit bodies
- Common on hardwoods

Destroying Angel
- Poisonous ☹
- White stalk and gills
- White cap or white edge and yellowish, pinkish, or tan center
- Egg-shaped cap

Chicken of the Woods
- Edible ☺
- Fan-shaped and suede-like texture
- Fruitbody with yellow, round pores
- Brownish color

Chanterelle
- Edible ☺
- Shape looks like bell of a trumpet
- Bright yellow/orange
- Similar look to Jack o'Lantern

Deadly Galerina
- Poisonous ☹
- Brownish, sticky cap, yellowish to rusty gills, ring on stalk
- Edges are curved against gills
- Gills narrow, crowded

Witches' Butter
- Edible ☺
- Small, yellow, irregularly lobed, gelatinous masses
- Grows on dead deciduous wood, especially oaks

Spore Print

Location

Site / GPS: _____ Date: _____

○ Living Tree   ○ Leaf Litter   ○ Mulch   ○ Dead Tree or Wood   ○ Grass
○ Soil   ○ Other _____

Type of Tree(s) On or Near: _____

Forest Type: ○ Deciduous   ○ Coniferous   ○ Tropical   ○ Other _____

Weather Conditions: _____

General

Size (overall height): _____   Color: _____   Spore Color: _____

Texture: ○ Tough   ○ Brittle   ○ Leathery   ○ Woody   ○ Soft   ○ Slimy
○ Spongy   ○ Powdery   ○ Waxy   ○ Rubbery   ○ Watery   (Other) _____

Bruising When Touched?   ○ Yes   ○ No   Notes: _____

Structures: ○ Cup   ○ Ring   ○ Warts   _____

Cap Characteristics

Campanulate
(bell-shaped)

Conical
(triangular)

Cylindrical
(shaped like half an egg)

Convex
(outwardly rounded)

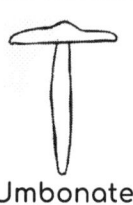

Flat
(with top of
uniform height)

Infundibuliform
(deeply, depressed,
funnel-shaped)

Depressed
(with a low
central region)

Umbonate
(with a central
bump or knob)

Surface Markings (warts, scales, slime, etc.): _____

Cap Margin: Smooth, Inrolled, Sinuous/Wavy, Other: _____

Color Changes: _____

Undercap

Gills ○

Attachment: Free or Decurrent

Spacing: Crowded, Close,
Distant, Subdistant

Color/Bruising: _____

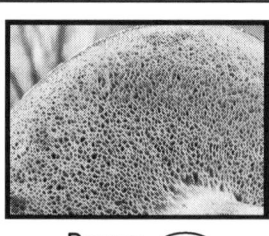

Pores ○

Color: _____

Pore Size: _____

Pore Pattern: _____

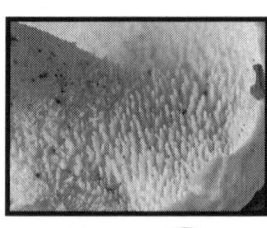

Teeth ○

Color: _____

Teeth Length: _____

Flesh: Soft or Tough

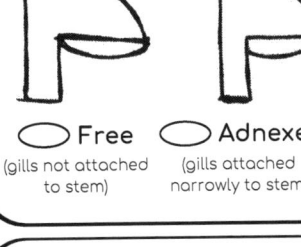

○ Free
(gills not attached to stem)

○ Adnexed
(gills attached narrowly to stem)

○ Sinuate
(gills smoothly notched and running briefly down stem)

○ Adnate
(gills widely attached widely to stem)

○ Descending
(gills running down stem for some length)

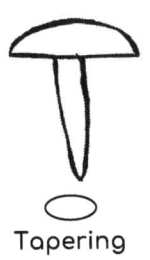

Tapering

Equal

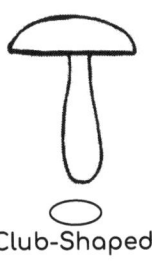

Club-Shaped

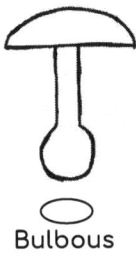

Bulbous

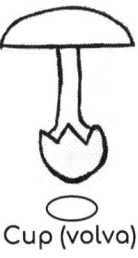

Cup (volva)

Morels

- Edible ☺
- Honeycombed cap
- Most morels cap is longer than stem
- Spore print is usually light colored
- Interior is hollow

Puffballs

- Edible ☺
- Color is white
- Rounded-shaped balls with or without spiny warts on top
- Can be mistaken for golf ball, baseball or even soccer ball

Fly Agaric

- Poisonous ☹
- Red-brown cap - irregularly lobed, like a brain
- Tube-like hollows
- Yellowish spore print
- Smooth with more wrinkles as it ages

Oyster Mushroom

- Edible ☺
- Grows on hardwood trees
- Gills descend to base
- Gills are not saw toothed or ruffled
- Spore deposit gray

Death Cap

- Poisonous ☹
- Flattened top
- White cap with brownish scales
- Gills are free and white, turning green as they mature

Jack O'Lantern

- Poisonous ☹
- Bright orange to yellowish
- Grows in clusters
- Cap convex
- Gills narrow
- Cream spore print

Lion's Mane

- Edible ☺
- Covered all over with long, spine-like hairs
- Club-shaped fruit bodies
- Common on hardwoods

Destroying Angel

- Poisonous ☹
- White stalk and gills
- White cap or white edge and yellowish, pinkish, or tan center
- Egg-shaped cap

Chicken of the Woods

- Edible ☺
- Fan-shaped and suede-like texture
- Fruitbody with yellow, round pores
- Brownish color

Chanterelle

- Edible ☺
- Shape looks like bell of a trumpet
- Bright yellow/orange
- Similar look to Jack o'Lantern

Deadly Galerina

- Poisonous ☹
- Brownish, sticky cap, yellowish to rusty gills, ring on stalk
- Edges are curved against gills
- Gills narrow, crowded

Witches' Butter

- Edible ☺
- Small, yellow, irregularly lobed, gelatinous masses
- Grows on dead deciduous wood, especially oaks

Spore Print

_____

_____

_____

_____

_____

_____

Location

Site / GPS: _____ Date: _____

◯ Living Tree   ◯ Leaf Litter   ◯ Mulch   ◯ Dead Tree or Wood   ◯ Grass
◯ Soil   ◯ Other _____

Type of Tree(s) On or Near: _____

Forest Type: ◯ Deciduous   ◯ Coniferous   ◯ Tropical   ◯ Other _____

Weather Conditions: _____

General

Size (overall height): _____ Color: _____ Spore Color: _____

Texture: ◯ Tough   ◯ Brittle   ◯ Leathery   ◯ Woody   ◯ Soft   ◯ Slimy
◯ Spongy   ◯ Powdery   ◯ Waxy   ◯ Rubbery   ◯ Watery   (Other) _____

Bruising When Touched? ◯ Yes   ◯ No   Notes: _____

Structures: ◯ Cup   ◯ Ring   ◯ Warts   _____

Cap Characteristics

Campanulate
(bell-shaped)

Conical
(triangular)

Cylindrical
(shaped like half an egg)

Convex
(outwardly rounded)

Flat
(with top of
uniform height)

Infundibuliform
(deeply, depressed,
funnel-shaped)

Depressed
(with a low
central region)

Umbonate
(with a central
bump or knob)

Surface Markings (warts, scales, slime, etc.): _____

Cap Margin: Smooth, Inrolled, Sinuous/Wavy, Other: _____

Color Changes: _____

Undercap

Gills ◯

Attachment: Free or Decurrent

Spacing: Crowded, Close,
Distant, Subdistant

Color/Bruising: _____

Pores ◯

Color: _____

Pore Size: _____

Pore Pattern: _____

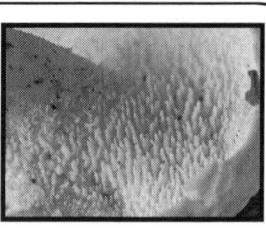

Teeth ◯

Color: _____

Teeth Length: _____

Flesh: Soft or Tough

○ **Free**
(gills not attached to stem)

○ **Adnexed**
(gills attached narrowly to stem)

○ **Sinuate**
(gills smoothly notched and running briefly down stem)

○ **Adnate**
(gills widely attached widely to stem)

○ **Descending**
(gills running down stem for some length)

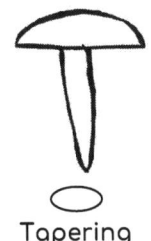  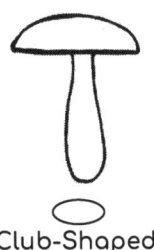 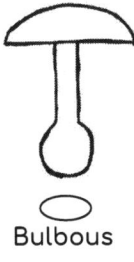 

○ **Tapering**   ○ **Equal**   ○ **Club-Shaped**   ○ **Bulbous**   ○ **Cup (volva)**

Morels
- Edible ☺
- Honeycombed cap
- Most morels cap is longer than stem
- Spore print is usually light colored
- Interior is hollow

Puffballs
- Edible ☺
- Color is white
- Rounded-shaped balls with or without spiny warts on top
- Can be mistaken for golf ball, baseball or even soccer ball

Fly Agaric
- Poisonous ☹
- Red-brown cap - irregularly lobed, like a brain
- Tube-like hollows
- Yellowish spore print
- Smooth with more wrinkles as it ages

Oyster Mushroom
- Edible ☺
- Grows on hardwood trees
- Gills descend to base
- Gills are not saw toothed or ruffled
- Spore deposit gray

Death Cap
- Poisonous ☹
- Flattened top
- White cap with brownish scales
- Gills are free and white, turning green as they mature

Jack O'Lantern
- Poisonous ☹
- Bright orange to yellowish
- Grows in clusters
- Cap convex
- Gills narrow
- Cream spore print

Lion's Mane
- Edible ☺
- Covered all over with long, spine-like hairs
- Club-shaped fruit bodies
- Common on hardwoods

Destroying Angel
- Poisonous ☹
- White stalk and gills
- White cap or white edge and yellowish, pinkish, or tan center
- Egg-shaped cap

Chicken of the Woods
- Edible ☺
- Fan-shaped and suede-like texture
- Fruitbody with yellow, round pores
- Brownish color

Chanterelle
- Edible ☺
- Shape looks like bell of a trumpet
- Bright yellow/orange
- Similar look to Jack o'Lantern

Deadly Galerina
- Poisonous ☹
- Brownish, sticky cap, yellowish to rusty gills, ring on stalk
- Edges are curved against gills
- Gills narrow, crowded

Witches' Butter
- Edible ☺
- Small, yellow, irregularly lobed, gelatinous masses
- Grows on dead deciduous wood, especially oaks

Spore Print

_____

_____

_____

_____

_____

_____

Location

Site / GPS: _____ Date: _____

○ Living Tree   ○ Leaf Litter   ○ Mulch   ○ Dead Tree or Wood   ○ Grass
○ Soil   ○ Other _____

Type of Tree(s) On or Near: _____

Forest Type: ○ Deciduous   ○ Coniferous   ○ Tropical   ○ Other _____

Weather Conditions: _____

General

Size (overall height): _____ Color: _____ Spore Color: _____

Texture: ○ Tough ○ Brittle ○ Leathery ○ Woody ○ Soft ○ Slimy
○ Spongy ○ Powdery ○ Waxy ○ Rubbery ○ Watery (Other) _____

Bruising When Touched? ○ Yes ○ No   Notes: _____

Structures: ○ Cup ○ Ring ○ Warts   _____

Cap Characteristics

Campanulate
(bell-shaped)

Conical
(triangular)

Cylindrical
(shaped like half an egg)

Convex
(outwardly rounded)

Flat
(with top of uniform height)

Infundibuliform
(deeply, depressed, funnel-shaped)

Depressed
(with a low central region)

Umbonate
(with a central bump or knob)

Surface Markings (warts, scales, slime, etc.): _____

Cap Margin: Smooth, Inrolled, Sinuous/Wavy, Other: _____

Color Changes: _____

Undercap

Gills ○
Attachment: Free or Decurrent
Spacing: Crowded, Close,
         Distant, Subdistant
Color/Bruising: _____

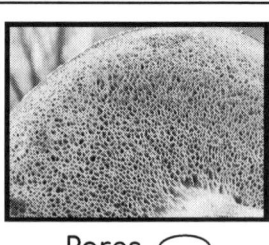

Pores ○
Color: _____
Pore Size: _____
Pore Pattern: _____

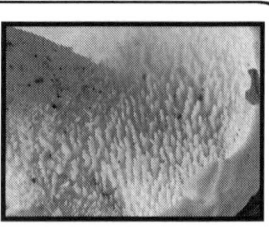

Teeth ○
Color: _____
Teeth Length: _____
Flesh: Soft or Tough

- **Free** (gills not attached to stem)
- **Adnexed** (gills attached narrowly to stem)
- **Sinuate** (gills smoothly notched and running briefly down stem)
- **Adnate** (gills widely attached widely to stem)
- **Descending** (gills running down stem for some length)

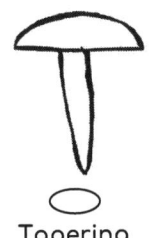  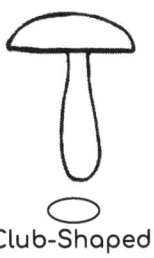 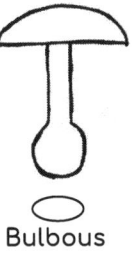  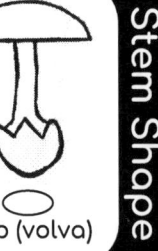

Tapering   **Equal**   **Club-Shaped**   **Bulbous**   **Cup (volva)**

Morels
- Edible ☺
- Honeycombed cap
- Most morels cap is longer than stem
- Spore print is usually light colored
- Interior is hollow

Puffballs
- Edible ☺
- Color is white
- Rounded-shaped balls with or without spiny warts on top
- Can be mistaken for golf ball, baseball or even soccer ball

Fly Agaric
- Poisonous ☹
- Red-brown cap - irregularly lobed, like a brain
- Tube-like hollows
- Yellowish spore print
- Smooth with more wrinkles as it ages

Oyster Mushroom
- Edible ☺
- Grows on hardwood trees
- Gills descend to base
- Gills are not saw toothed or ruffled
- Spore deposit gray

Death Cap
- Poisonous ☹
- Flattened top
- White cap with brownish scales
- Gills are free and white, turning green as they mature

Jack O'Lantern
- Poisonous ☹
- Bright orange to yellowish
- Grows in clusters
- Cap convex
- Gills narrow
- Cream spore print

Lion's Mane
- Edible ☺
- Covered all over with long, spine-like hairs
- Club-shaped fruit bodies
- Common on hardwoods

Destroying Angel
- Poisonous ☹
- White stalk and gills
- White cap or white edge and yellowish, pinkish, or tan center
- Egg-shaped cap

Chicken of the Woods
- Edible ☺
- Fan-shaped and suede-like texture
- Fruitbody with yellow, round pores
- Brownish color

Chanterelle
- Edible ☺
- Shape looks like bell of a trumpet
- Bright yellow/orange
- Similar look to Jack o'Lantern

Deadly Galerina
- Poisonous ☹
- Brownish, sticky cap, yellowish to rusty gills, ring on stalk
- Edges are curved against gills
- Gills narrow, crowded

Witches' Butter
- Edible ☺
- Small, yellow, irregularly lobed, gelatinous masses
- Grows on dead deciduous wood, especially oaks

Spore Print

Location

Site / GPS: _____ Date: _____

○ Living Tree ○ Leaf Litter ○ Mulch ○ Dead Tree or Wood ○ Grass
○ Soil ○ Other _____

Type of Tree(s) On or Near: _____

Forest Type: ○ Deciduous ○ Coniferous ○ Tropical ○ Other _____

Weather Conditions: _____

General

Size (overall height): _____ Color: _____ Spore Color: _____

Texture: ○ Tough ○ Brittle ○ Leathery ○ Woody ○ Soft ○ Slimy
○ Spongy ○ Powdery ○ Waxy ○ Rubbery ○ Watery (Other) _____

Bruising When Touched? ○ Yes ○ No   Notes: _____

Structures: ○ Cup ○ Ring ○ Warts   _____

Cap Characteristics

Campanulate
(bell-shaped)

Conical
(triangular)

Cylindrical
(shaped like half an egg)

Convex
(outwardly rounded)

Flat
(with top of
uniform height)

Infundibuliform
(deeply, depressed,
funnel-shaped)

Depressed
(with a low
central region)

Umbonate
(with a central
bump or knob)

Surface Markings (warts, scales, slime, etc.): _____

Cap Margin: Smooth, Inrolled, Sinuous/Wavy, Other: _____

Color Changes: _____

Undercap

Gills ○

Attachment: Free or Decurrent

Spacing: Crowded, Close,
            Distant, Subdistant

Color/Bruising: _____

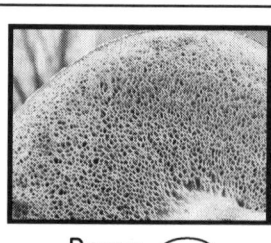

Pores ○

Color: _____

Pore Size: _____

Pore Pattern: _____

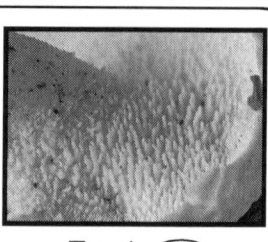

Teeth ○

Color: _____

Teeth Length: _____

Flesh: Soft or Tough

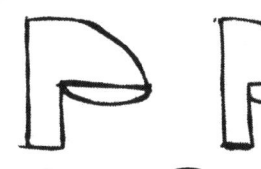

 Free
(gills not attached
to stem)

 Adnexed
(gills attached
narrowly to stem)

 Sinuate
(gills smoothly notched
and running
briefly down stem)

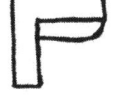 Adnate
(gills widely attached
widely to stem)

 Descending
(gills running down
stem for some length)

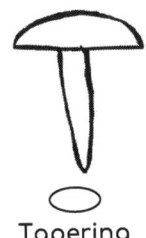 Tapering

 Equal

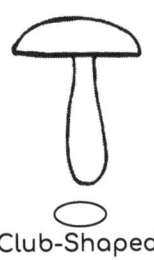 Club-Shaped

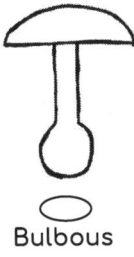 Bulbous

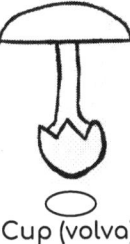 Cup (volva)

Morels
- Edible ☺
- Honeycombed cap
- Most morels cap is longer than stem
- Spore print is usually light colored
- Interior is hollow

Puffballs
- Edible ☺
- Color is white
- Rounded-shaped balls with or without spiny warts on top
- Can be mistaken for golf ball, baseball or even soccer ball

Fly Agaric
- Poisonous ☹
- Red-brown cap - irregularly lobed, like a brain
- Tube-like hollows
- Yellowish spore print
- Smooth with more wrinkles as it ages

Oyster Mushroom
- Edible ☺
- Grows on hardwood trees
- Gills descend to base
- Gills are not saw toothed or ruffled
- Spore deposit gray

Death Cap
- Poisonous ☹
- Flattened top
- White cap with brownish scales
- Gills are free and white, turning green as they mature

Jack O'Lantern
- Poisonous ☹
- Bright orange to yellowish
- Grows in clusters
- Cap convex
- Gills narrow
- Cream spore print

Lion's Mane
- Edible ☺
- Covered all over with long, spine-like hairs
- Club-shaped fruit bodies
- Common on hardwoods

Destroying Angel
- Poisonous ☹
- White stalk and gills
- White cap or white edge and yellowish, pinkish, or tan center
- Egg-shaped cap

Chicken of the Woods
- Edible ☺
- Fan-shaped and suede-like texture
- Fruitbody with yellow, round pores
- Brownish color

Chanterelle
- Edible ☺
- Shape looks like bell of a trumpet
- Bright yellow/orange
- Similar look to Jack o'Lantern

Deadly Galerina
- Poisonous ☹
- Brownish, sticky cap, yellowish to rusty gills, ring on stalk
- Edges are curved against gills
- Gills narrow, crowded

Witches' Butter
- Edible ☺
- Small, yellow, irregularly lobed, gelatinous masses
- Grows on dead deciduous wood, especially oaks

Spore Print

Location

Site / GPS: _____ Date: _____

○ Living Tree ○ Leaf Litter ○ Mulch ○ Dead Tree or Wood ○ Grass
○ Soil ○ Other _____

Type of Tree(s) On or Near: _____

Forest Type: ○ Deciduous ○ Coniferous ○ Tropical ○ Other _____

Weather Conditions: _____

General

Size (overall height): _____ Color: _____ Spore Color: _____

Texture: ○ Tough ○ Brittle ○ Leathery ○ Woody ○ Soft ○ Slimy
○ Spongy ○ Powdery ○ Waxy ○ Rubbery ○ Watery (Other) _____

Bruising When Touched? ○ Yes ○ No   Notes: _____

Structures: ○ Cup ○ Ring ○ Warts   _____

Cap Characteristics

Campanulate
(bell-shaped)

Conical
(triangular)

Cylindrical
(shaped like half an egg)

Convex
(outwardly rounded)

Flat
(with top of
uniform height)

Infundibuliform
(deeply, depressed,
funnel-shaped)

Depressed
(with a low
central region)

Umbonate
(with a central
bump or knob)

Surface Markings (warts, scales, slime, etc.): _____

Cap Margin: Smooth, Inrolled, Sinuous/Wavy, Other: _____

Color Changes: _____

Undercap

Gills ○
Attachment: Free or Decurrent
Spacing: Crowded, Close,
Distant, Subdistant
Color/Bruising: _____

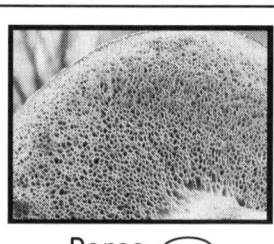

Pores ○
Color: _____
Pore Size: _____
Pore Pattern: _____

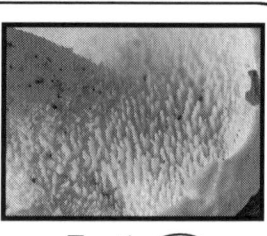

Teeth ○
Color: _____
Teeth Length: _____
Flesh: Soft or Tough

◯ Free
(gills not attached to stem)

◯ Adnexed
(gills attached narrowly to stem)

◯ Sinuate
(gills smoothly notched and running briefly down stem)

◯ Adnate
(gills widely attached widely to stem)

◯ Descending
(gills running down stem for some length)

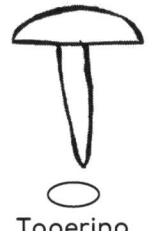  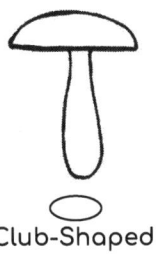 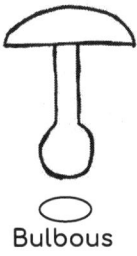 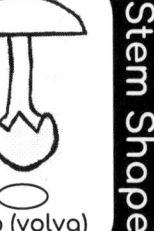

Tapering

Equal

Club-Shaped

Bulbous

Cup (volva)

Morels
- Edible ☺
- Honeycombed cap
- Most morels cap is longer than stem
- Spore print is usually light colored
- Interior is hollow

Puffballs
- Edible ☺
- Color is white
- Rounded-shaped balls with or without spiny warts on top
- Can be mistaken for golf ball, baseball or even soccer ball

Fly Agaric
- Poisonous ☹
- Red-brown cap - irregularly lobed, like a brain
- Tube-like hollows
- Yellowish spore print
- Smooth with more wrinkles as it ages

Oyster Mushroom
- Edible ☺
- Grows on hardwood trees
- Gills descend to base
- Gills are not saw toothed or ruffled
- Spore deposit gray

Death Cap
- Poisonous ☹
- Flattened top
- White cap with brownish scales
- Gills are free and white, turning green as they mature

Jack O'Lantern
- Poisonous ☹
- Bright orange to yellowish
- Grows in clusters
- Cap convex
- Gills narrow
- Cream spore print

Lion's Mane
- Edible ☺
- Covered all over with long, spine-like hairs
- Club-shaped fruit bodies
- Common on hardwoods

Destroying Angel
- Poisonous ☹
- White stalk and gills
- White cap or white edge and yellowish, pinkish, or tan center
- Egg-shaped cap

Chicken of the Woods
- Edible ☺
- Fan-shaped and suede-like texture
- Fruitbody with yellow, round pores
- Brownish color

Chanterelle
- Edible ☺
- Shape looks like bell of a trumpet
- Bright yellow/orange
- Similar look to Jack o'Lantern

Deadly Galerina
- Poisonous ☹
- Brownish, sticky cap, yellowish to rusty gills, ring on stalk
- Edges are curved against gills
- Gills narrow, crowded

Witches' Butter
- Edible ☺
- Small, yellow, irregularly lobed, gelatinous masses
- Grows on dead deciduous wood, especially oaks

Spore Print

Location

Site / GPS: _____ Date: _____

○ Living Tree   ○ Leaf Litter   ○ Mulch   ○ Dead Tree or Wood   ○ Grass
○ Soil   ○ Other _____

Type of Tree(s) On or Near: _____

Forest Type: ○ Deciduous   ○ Coniferous   ○ Tropical   ○ Other _____

Weather Conditions: _____

General

Size (overall height): _____   Color: _____   Spore Color: _____

Texture: ○ Tough ○ Brittle ○ Leathery ○ Woody ○ Soft ○ Slimy
○ Spongy ○ Powdery ○ Waxy ○ Rubbery ○ Watery (Other) _____

Bruising When Touched? ○ Yes ○ No   Notes: _____

Structures: ○ Cup   ○ Ring   ○ Warts   _____

Cap Characteristics

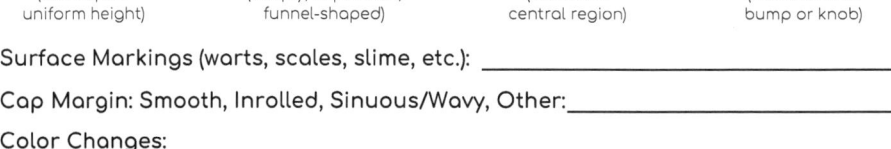

Campanulate
(bell-shaped)

Conical
(triangular)

Cylindrical
(shaped like half an egg)

Convex
(outwardly rounded)

Flat
(with top of
uniform height)

Infundibuliform
(deeply, depressed,
funnel-shaped)

Depressed
(with a low
central region)

Umbonate
(with a central
bump or knob)

Surface Markings (warts, scales, slime, etc.): _____

Cap Margin: Smooth, Inrolled, Sinuous/Wavy, Other:_____

Color Changes: _____

Undercap

Gills ○

Attachment: Free or Decurrent

Spacing: Crowded, Close,
        Distant, Subdistant

Color/Bruising: _____

Pores ○

Color: _____

Pore Size: _____

Pore Pattern: _____

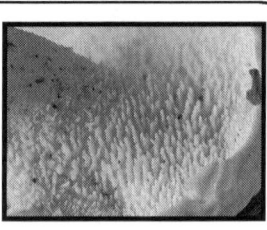

Teeth ○

Color: _____

Teeth Length: _____

Flesh: Soft or Tough

○ Free
(gills not attached to stem)

○ Adnexed
(gills attached narrowly to stem)

○ Sinuate
(gills smoothly notched and running briefly down stem)

○ Adnate
(gills widely attached widely to stem)

○ Descenting
(gills running down stem for some length)

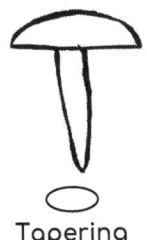 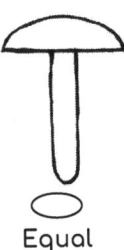 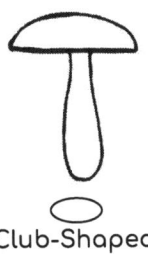 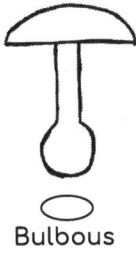 

○ Tapering

○ Equal

○ Club-Shaped

○ Bulbous

○ Cup (volva)

Morels

- Edible ☺
- Honeycombed cap
- Most morels cap is longer than stem
- Spore print is usually light colored
- Interior is hollow

Puffballs

- Edible ☺
- Color is white
- Rounded-shaped balls with or without spiny warts on top
- Can be mistaken for golf ball, baseball or even soccer ball

Fly Agaric

- Poisonous ☹
- Red-brown cap - irregularly lobed, like a brain
- Tube-like hollows
- Yellowish spore print
- Smooth with more wrinkles as it ages

Oyster Mushroom

- Edible ☺
- Grows on hardwood trees
- Gills descend to base
- Gills are not saw toothed or ruffled
- Spore deposit gray

Death Cap

- Poisonous ☹
- Flattened top
- White cap with brownish scales
- Gills are free and white, turning green as they mature

Jack O'Lantern

- Poisonous ☹
- Bright orange to yellowish
- Grows in clusters
- Cap convex
- Gills narrow
- Cream spore print

Lion's Mane

- Edible ☺
- Covered all over with long, spine-like hairs
- Club-shaped fruit bodies
- Common on hardwoods

Destroying Angel

- Poisonous ☹
- White stalk and gills
- White cap or white edge and yellowish, pinkish, or tan center
- Egg-shaped cap

Chicken of the Woods

- Edible ☺
- Fan-shaped and suede-like texture
- Fruitbody with yellow, round pores
- Brownish color

Chanterelle

- Edible ☺
- Shape looks like bell of a trumpet
- Bright yellow/orange
- Similar look to Jack o'Lantern

Deadly Galerina

- Poisonous ☹
- Brownish, sticky cap, yellowish to rusty gills, ring on stalk
- Edges are curved against gills
- Gills narrow, crowded

Witches' Butter

- Edible ☺
- Small, yellow, irregularly lobed, gelatinous masses
- Grows on dead deciduous wood, especially oaks

Spore Print

_____
_____
_____
_____
_____
_____

Location

Site / GPS: _____ Date: _____

○ Living Tree ○ Leaf Litter ○ Mulch ○ Dead Tree or Wood ○ Grass
○ Soil ○ Other _____

Type of Tree(s) On or Near: _____

Forest Type: ○ Deciduous ○ Coniferous ○ Tropical ○ Other _____

Weather Conditions: _____

General

Size (overall height): _____ Color: _____ Spore Color: _____

Texture: ○ Tough ○ Brittle ○ Leathery ○ Woody ○ Soft ○ Slimy
○ Spongy ○ Powdery ○ Waxy ○ Rubbery ○ Watery (Other) _____

Bruising When Touched? ○ Yes ○ No   Notes: _____

Structures: ○ Cup ○ Ring ○ Warts   _____

Cap Characteristics

Campanulate
(bell-shaped)

Conical
(triangular)

Cylindrical
(shaped like half an egg)

Convex
(outwardly rounded)

Flat
(with top of
uniform height)

Infundibuliform
(deeply, depressed,
funnel-shaped)

Depressed
(with a low
central region)

Umbonate
(with a central
bump or knob)

Surface Markings (warts, scales, slime, etc.): _____

Cap Margin: Smooth, Inrolled, Sinuous/Wavy, Other: _____

Color Changes: _____

Undercap

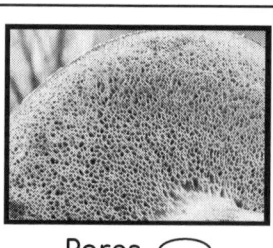

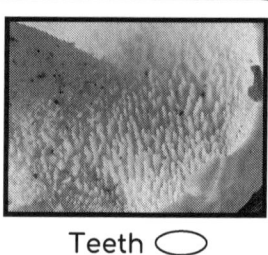

Gills ○

Attachment: Free or Decurrent

Spacing: Crowded, Close,
Distant, Subdistant

Color/Bruising: _____

Pores ○

Color: _____

Pore Size: _____

Pore Pattern: _____

Teeth ○

Color: _____

Teeth Length: _____

Flesh: Soft or Tough

Free	Adnexed	Sinuate	Adnate	Descending
(gills not attached to stem)	(gills attached narrowly to stem)	(gills smoothly notched and running briefly down stem)	(gills widely attached widely to stem)	(gills running down stem for some length)

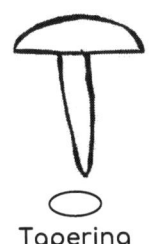  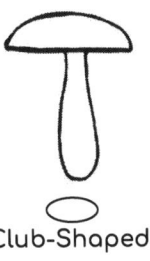 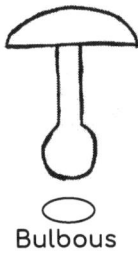 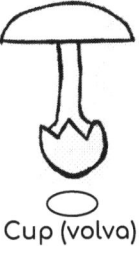

Tapering	Equal	Club-Shaped	Bulbous	Cup (volva)

Morels
- Edible ☺
- Honeycombed cap
- Most morels cap is longer than stem
- Spore print is usually light colored
- Interior is hollow

Puffballs
- Edible ☺
- Color is white
- Rounded-shaped balls with or without spiny warts on top
- Can be mistaken for golf ball, baseball or even soccer ball

Fly Agaric
- Poisonous ☹
- Red-brown cap - irregularly lobed, like a brain
- Tube-like hollows
- Yellowish spore print
- Smooth with more wrinkles as it ages

Oyster Mushroom
- Edible ☺
- Grows on hardwood trees
- Gills descend to base
- Gills are not saw toothed or ruffled
- Spore deposit gray

Death Cap
- Poisonous ☹
- Flattened top
- White cap with brownish scales
- Gills are free and white, turning green as they mature

Jack O'Lantern
- Poisonous ☹
- Bright orange to yellowish
- Grows in clusters
- Cap convex
- Gills narrow
- Cream spore print

Lion's Mane
- Edible ☺
- Covered all over with long, spine-like hairs
- Club-shaped fruit bodies
- Common on hardwoods

Destroying Angel
- Poisonous ☹
- White stalk and gills
- White cap or white edge and yellowish, pinkish, or tan center
- Egg-shaped cap

Chicken of the Woods
- Edible ☺
- Fan-shaped and suede-like texture
- Fruitbody with yellow, round pores
- Brownish color

Chanterelle
- Edible ☺
- Shape looks like bell of a trumpet
- Bright yellow/orange
- Similar look to Jack o'Lantern

Deadly Galerina
- Poisonous ☹
- Brownish, sticky cap, yellowish to rusty gills, ring on stalk
- Edges are curved against gills
- Gills narrow, crowded

Witches' Butter
- Edible ☺
- Small, yellow, irregularly lobed, gelatinous masses
- Grows on dead deciduous wood, especially oaks

Spore Print

Location

Site / GPS: _____ Date: _____

○ Living Tree ○ Leaf Litter ○ Mulch ○ Dead Tree or Wood ○ Grass

○ Soil ○ Other _____

Type of Tree(s) On or Near: _____

Forest Type: ○ Deciduous ○ Coniferous ○ Tropical ○ Other _____

Weather Conditions: _____

General

Size (overall height): _____ Color: _____ Spore Color: _____

Texture: ○ Tough ○ Brittle ○ Leathery ○ Woody ○ Soft ○ Slimy

○ Spongy ○ Powdery ○ Waxy ○ Rubbery ○ Watery (Other) _____

Bruising When Touched? ○ Yes ○ No   Notes: _____

Structures: ○ Cup ○ Ring ○ Warts   _____

Cap Characteristics

Campanulate
(bell-shaped)

Conical
(triangular)

Cylindrical
(shaped like half an egg)

Convex
(outwardly rounded)

Flat
(with top of
uniform height)

Infundibuliform
(deeply, depressed,
funnel-shaped)

Depressed
(with a low
central region)

Umbonate
(with a central
bump or knob)

Surface Markings (warts, scales, slime, etc.): _____

Cap Margin: Smooth, Inrolled, Sinuous/Wavy, Other: _____

Color Changes: _____

Undercap

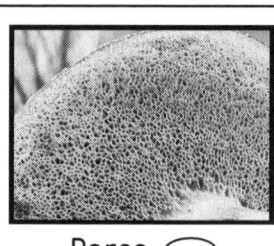

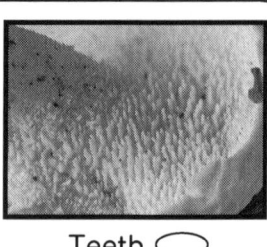

Gills ○

Attachment: Free or Decurrent

Spacing: Crowded, Close,
Distant, Subdistant

Color/Bruising: _____

Pores ○

Color: _____

Pore Size: _____

Pore Pattern: _____

Teeth ○

Color: _____

Teeth Length: _____

Flesh: Soft or Tough

Gill Attachment

- ○ **Free** (gills not attached to stem)
- ○ **Adnexed** (gills attached narrowly to stem)
- ○ **Sinuate** (gills smoothly notched and running briefly down stem)
- ○ **Adnate** (gills widely attached widely to stem)
- ○ **Descending** (gills running down stem for some length)

Stem Shape

- ○ **Tapering**
- ○ **Equal**
- ○ **Club-Shaped**
- ○ **Bulbous**
- ○ **Cup (volva)**

Common Mushrooms

Morels
- Edible ☺
- Honeycombed cap
- Most morels cap is longer than stem
- Spore print is usually light colored
- Interior is hollow

Oyster Mushroom
- Edible ☺
- Grows on hardwood trees
- Gills descend to base
- Gills are not saw toothed or ruffled
- Spore deposit gray

Lion's Mane
- Edible ☺
- Covered all over with long, spine-like hairs
- Club-shaped fruit bodies
- Common on hardwoods

Chanterelle
- Edible ☺
- Shape looks like bell of a trumpet
- Bright yellow/orange
- Similar look to Jack o'Lantern

Puffballs
- Edible ☺
- Color is white
- Rounded-shaped balls with or without spiny warts on top
- Can be mistaken for golf ball, baseball or even soccer ball

Death Cap
- Poisonous ☹
- Flattened top
- White cap with brownish scales
- Gills are free and white, turning green as they mature

Destroying Angel
- Poisonous ☹
- White stalk and gills
- White cap or white edge and yellowish, pinkish, or tan center
- Egg-shaped cap

Deadly Galerina
- Poisonous ☹
- Brownish, sticky cap, yellowish to rusty gills, ring on stalk
- Edges are curved against gills
- Gills narrow, crowded

Fly Agaric
- Poisonous ☹
- Red-brown cap - irregularly lobed, like a brain
- Tube-like hollows
- Yellowish spore print
- Smooth with more wrinkles as it ages

Jack O'Lantern
- Poisonous ☹
- Bright orange to yellowish
- Grows in clusters
- Cap convex
- Gills narrow
- Cream spore print

Chicken of the Woods
- Edible ☺
- Fan-shaped and suede-like texture
- Fruitbody with yellow, round pores
- Brownish color

Witches' Butter
- Edible ☺
- Small, yellow, irregularly lobed, gelatinous masses
- Grows on dead deciduous wood, especially oaks

Notes

Spore Print

_____

_____

_____

_____

_____

_____

Location

Site / GPS: _____ Date: _____

○ Living Tree ○ Leaf Litter ○ Mulch ○ Dead Tree or Wood ○ Grass
○ Soil ○ Other _____

Type of Tree(s) On or Near: _____

Forest Type: ○ Deciduous ○ Coniferous ○ Tropical ○ Other _____

Weather Conditions: _____

General

Size (overall height): _____ Color: _____ Spore Color: _____

Texture: ○ Tough ○ Brittle ○ Leathery ○ Woody ○ Soft ○ Slimy
○ Spongy ○ Powdery ○ Waxy ○ Rubbery ○ Watery (Other) _____

Bruising When Touched? ○ Yes ○ No   Notes: _____

Structures: ○ Cup ○ Ring ○ Warts   _____

Cap Characteristics

Campanulate
(bell-shaped)

Conical
(triangular)

Cylindrical
(shaped like half an egg)

Convex
(outwardly rounded)

Flat
(with top of
uniform height)

Infundibuliform
(deeply, depressed,
funnel-shaped)

Depressed
(with a low
central region)

Umbonate
(with a central
bump or knob)

Surface Markings (warts, scales, slime, etc.): _____

Cap Margin: Smooth, Inrolled, Sinuous/Wavy, Other:_____

Color Changes: _____

Undercap

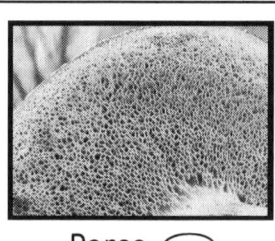

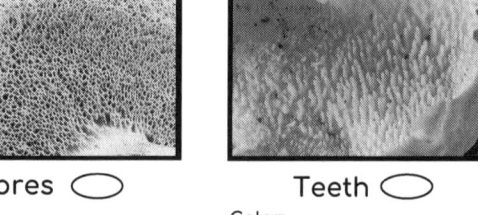

Gills ○

Attachment: Free or Decurrent

Spacing: Crowded, Close,
Distant, Subdistant

Color/Bruising: _____

Pores ○

Color: _____

Pore Size: _____

Pore Pattern: _____

Teeth ○

Color: _____

Teeth Length: _____

Flesh: Soft or Tough

◯ Free
(gills not attached to stem)

◯ Adnexed
(gills attached narrowly to stem)

◯ Sinuate
(gills smoothly notched and running briefly down stem)

◯ Adnate
(gills widely attached widely to stem)

◯ Descenting
(gills running down stem for some length)

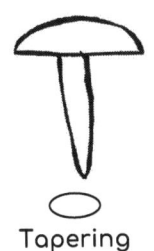  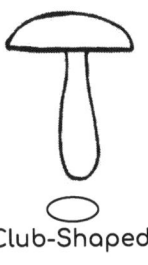 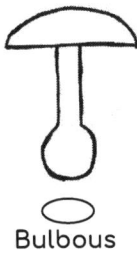 

◯ Tapering

◯ Equal

◯ Club-Shaped

◯ Bulbous

◯ Cup (volva)

Morels
- Edible ☺
- Honeycombed cap
- Most morels cap is longer than stem
- Spore print is usually light colored
- Interior is hollow

Puffballs
- Edible ☺
- Color is white
- Rounded-shaped balls with or without spiny warts on top
- Can be mistaken for golf ball, baseball or even soccer ball

Fly Agaric
- Poisonous ☹
- Red-brown cap - irregularly lobed, like a brain
- Tube-like hollows
- Yellowish spore print
- Smooth with more wrinkles as it ages

Oyster Mushroom
- Edible ☺
- Grows on hardwood trees
- Gills descend to base
- Gills are not saw toothed or ruffled
- Spore deposit gray

Death Cap
- Poisonous ☹
- Flattened top
- White cap with brownish scales
- Gills are free and white, turning green as they mature

Jack O'Lantern
- Poisonous ☹
- Bright orange to yellowish
- Grows in clusters
- Cap convex
- Gills narrow
- Cream spore print

Lion's Mane
- Edible ☺
- Covered all over with long, spine-like hairs
- Club-shaped fruit bodies
- Common on hardwoods

Destroying Angel
- Poisonous ☹
- White stalk and gills
- White cap or white edge and yellowish, pinkish, or tan center
- Egg-shaped cap

Chicken of the Woods
- Edible ☺
- Fan-shaped and suede-like texture
- Fruitbody with yellow, round pores
- Brownish color

Chanterelle
- Edible ☺
- Shape looks like bell of a trumpet
- Bright yellow/orange
- Similar look to Jack o'Lantern

Deadly Galerina
- Poisonous ☹
- Brownish, sticky cap, yellowish to rusty gills, ring on stalk
- Edges are curved against gills
- Gills narrow, crowded

Witches' Butter
- Edible ☺
- Small, yellow, irregularly lobed, gelatinous masses
- Grows on dead deciduous wood, especially oaks

Spore Print

_____

_____

_____

_____

_____

_____

Location

Site / GPS: _____ Date: _____

◯ Living Tree ◯ Leaf Litter ◯ Mulch ◯ Dead Tree or Wood ◯ Grass
◯ Soil ◯ Other _____

Type of Tree(s) On or Near: _____

Forest Type: ◯ Deciduous ◯ Coniferous ◯ Tropical ◯ Other _____

Weather Conditions: _____

General

Size (overall height): _____ Color: _____ Spore Color: _____

Texture: ◯ Tough ◯ Brittle ◯ Leathery ◯ Woody ◯ Soft ◯ Slimy
◯ Spongy ◯ Powdery ◯ Waxy ◯ Rubbery ◯ Watery (Other) _____

Bruising When Touched? ◯ Yes ◯ No   Notes: _____

Structures: ◯ Cup ◯ Ring ◯ Warts   _____

Cap Characteristics

Campanulate
(bell-shaped)

Conical
(triangular)

Cylindrical
(shaped like half an egg)

Convex
(outwardly rounded)

Flat
(with top of
uniform height)

Infundibuliform
(deeply, depressed,
funnel-shaped)

Depressed
(with a low
central region)

Umbonate
(with a central
bump or knob)

Surface Markings (warts, scales, slime, etc.): _____

Cap Margin: Smooth, Inrolled, Sinuous/Wavy, Other:_____

Color Changes: _____

Undercap

Gills ◯

Attachment: Free or Decurrent

Spacing: Crowded, Close,
        Distant, Subdistant

Color/Bruising: _____

Pores ◯

Color: _____

Pore Size: _____

Pore Pattern: _____

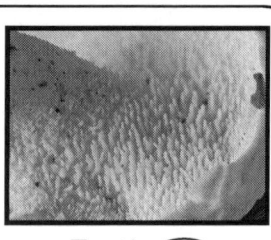

Teeth ◯

Color: _____

Teeth Length: _____

Flesh: Soft or Tough

Free	Adnexed	Sinuate	Adnate	Descending
(gills not attached to stem)	(gills attached narrowly to stem)	(gills smoothly notched and running briefly down stem)	(gills widely attached widely to stem)	(gills running down stem for some length)

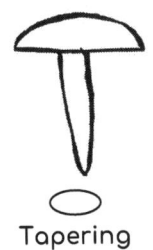  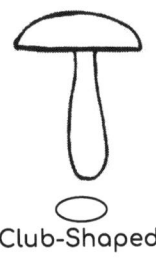 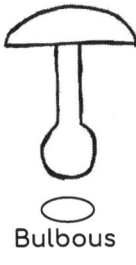 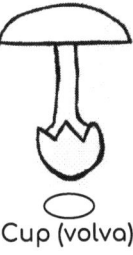 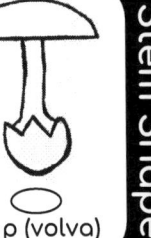

Tapering	Equal	Club-Shaped	Bulbous	Cup (volva)

Morels

- Edible ☺
- Honeycombed cap
- Most morels cap is longer than stem
- Spore print is usually light colored
- Interior is hollow

Puffballs

- Edible ☺
- Color is white
- Rounded-shaped balls with or without spiny warts on top
- Can be mistaken for golf ball, baseball or even soccer ball

Fly Agaric

- Poisonous ☹
- Red-brown cap - irregularly lobed, like a brain
- Tube-like hollows
- Yellowish spore print
- Smooth with more wrinkles as it ages

Oyster Mushroom

- Edible ☺
- Grows on hardwood trees
- Gills descend to base
- Gills are not saw toothed or ruffled
- Spore deposit gray

Death Cap

- Poisonous ☹
- Flattened top
- White cap with brownish scales
- Gills are free and white, turning green as they mature

Jack O'Lantern

- Poisonous ☹
- Bright orange to yellowish
- Grows in clusters
- Cap convex
- Gills narrow
- Cream spore print

Lion's Mane

- Edible ☺
- Covered all over with long, spine-like hairs
- Club-shaped fruit bodies
- Common on hardwoods

Destroying Angel

- Poisonous ☹
- White stalk and gills
- White cap or white edge and yellowish, pinkish, or tan center
- Egg-shaped cap

Chicken of the Woods

- Edible ☺
- Fan-shaped and suede-like texture
- Fruitbody with yellow, round pores
- Brownish color

Chanterelle

- Edible ☺
- Shape looks like bell of a trumpet
- Bright yellow/orange
- Similar look to Jack o'Lantern

Deadly Galerina

- Poisonous ☹
- Brownish, sticky cap, yellowish to rusty gills, ring on stalk
- Edges are curved against gills
- Gills narrow, crowded

Witches' Butter

- Edible ☺
- Small, yellow, irregularly lobed, gelatinous masses
- Grows on dead deciduous wood, especially oaks

Spore Print

Location

Site / GPS: _____ Date: _____

○ Living Tree   ○ Leaf Litter   ○ Mulch   ○ Dead Tree or Wood   ○ Grass
○ Soil   ○ Other _____

Type of Tree(s) On or Near: _____

Forest Type: ○ Deciduous   ○ Coniferous   ○ Tropical   ○ Other _____

Weather Conditions: _____

General

Size (overall height): _____   Color: _____   Spore Color: _____

Texture: ○ Tough   ○ Brittle   ○ Leathery   ○ Woody   ○ Soft   ○ Slimy
○ Spongy   ○ Powdery   ○ Waxy   ○ Rubbery   ○ Watery   (Other) _____

Bruising When Touched? ○ Yes   ○ No   Notes: _____

Structures: ○ Cup   ○ Ring   ○ Warts   _____

Cap Characteristics

Campanulate
(bell-shaped)

Conical
(triangular)

Cylindrical
(shaped like half an egg)

Convex
(outwardly rounded)

Flat
(with top of
uniform height)

Infundibuliform
(deeply, depressed,
funnel-shaped)

Depressed
(with a low
central region)

Umbonate
(with a central
bump or knob)

Surface Markings (warts, scales, slime, etc.): _____

Cap Margin: Smooth, Inrolled, Sinuous/Wavy, Other: _____

Color Changes: _____

Undercap

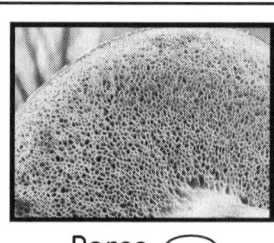

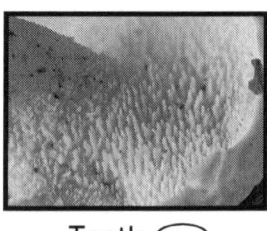

Gills ○

Attachment: Free or Decurrent

Spacing: Crowded, Close,
Distant, Subdistant

Color/Bruising: _____

Pores ○

Color: _____

Pore Size: _____

Pore Pattern: _____

Teeth ○

Color: _____

Teeth Length: _____

Flesh: Soft or Tough

○ **Free**
(gills not attached to stem)

○ **Adnexed**
(gills attached narrowly to stem)

○ **Sinuate**
(gills smoothly notched and running briefly down stem)

○ **Adnate**
(gills widely attached widely to stem)

○ **Descending**
(gills running down stem for some length)

Tapering

Equal

Club-Shaped

Bulbous

Cup (volva)

Morels

- Edible ☺
- Honeycombed cap
- Most morels cap is longer than stem
- Spore print is usually light colored
- Interior is hollow

Puffballs

- Edible ☺
- Color is white
- Rounded-shaped balls with or without spiny warts on top
- Can be mistaken for golf ball, baseball or even soccer ball

Fly Agaric

- Poisonous ☹
- Red-brown cap - irregularly lobed, like a brain
- Tube-like hollows
- Yellowish spore print
- Smooth with more wrinkles as it ages

Oyster Mushroom

- Edible ☺
- Grows on hardwood trees
- Gills descend to base
- Gills are not saw toothed or ruffled
- Spore deposit gray

Death Cap

- Poisonous ☹
- Flattened top
- White cap with brownish scales
- Gills are free and white, turning green as they mature

Jack O'Lantern

- Poisonous ☹
- Bright orange to yellowish
- Grows in clusters
- Cap convex
- Gills narrow
- Cream spore print

Lion's Mane

- Edible ☺
- Covered all over with long, spine-like hairs
- Club-shaped fruit bodies
- Common on hardwoods

Destroying Angel

- Poisonous ☹
- White stalk and gills
- White cap or white edge and yellowish, pinkish, or tan center
- Egg-shaped cap

Chicken of the Woods

- Edible ☺
- Fan-shaped and suede-like texture
- Fruitbody with yellow, round pores
- Brownish color

Chanterelle

- Edible ☺
- Shape looks like bell of a trumpet
- Bright yellow/orange
- Similar look to Jack o'Lantern

Deadly Galerina

- Poisonous ☹
- Brownish, sticky cap, yellowish to rusty gills, ring on stalk
- Edges are curved against gills
- Gills narrow, crowded

Witches' Butter

- Edible ☺
- Small, yellow, irregularly lobed, gelatinous masses
- Grows on dead deciduous wood, especially oaks

Spore Print

Location

Site / GPS: _____ Date: _____

○ Living Tree   ○ Leaf Litter   ○ Mulch   ○ Dead Tree or Wood   ○ Grass
○ Soil   ○ Other _____

Type of Tree(s) On or Near: _____

Forest Type: ○ Deciduous   ○ Coniferous   ○ Tropical   ○ Other _____

Weather Conditions: _____

General

Size (overall height): _____   Color: _____   Spore Color: _____

Texture: ○ Tough ○ Brittle ○ Leathery ○ Woody ○ Soft ○ Slimy
○ Spongy   ○ Powdery   ○ Waxy   ○ Rubbery   ○ Watery (Other) _____

Bruising When Touched? ○ Yes ○ No   Notes: _____

Structures: ○ Cup ○ Ring ○ Warts   _____

Cap Characteristics

Campanulate
(bell-shaped)

Conical
(triangular)

Cylindrical
(shaped like half an egg)

Convex
(outwardly rounded)

Flat
(with top of
uniform height)

Infundibuliform
(deeply, depressed,
funnel-shaped)

Depressed
(with a low
central region)

Umbonate
(with a central
bump or knob)

Surface Markings (warts, scales, slime, etc.): _____

Cap Margin: Smooth, Inrolled, Sinuous/Wavy, Other: _____

Color Changes: _____

Undercap

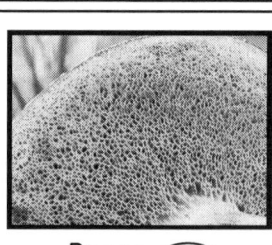

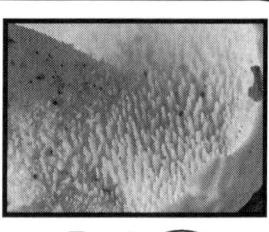

Gills ○

Attachment: Free or Decurrent

Spacing: Crowded, Close,
Distant, Subdistant

Color/Bruising: _____

Pores ○

Color: _____

Pore Size: _____

Pore Pattern: _____

Teeth ○

Color: _____

Teeth Length: _____

Flesh: Soft or Tough

 Free
(gills not attached to stem)

 Adnexed
(gills attached narrowly to stem)

Sinuate
(gills smoothly notched and running briefly down stem)

Adnate
(gills widely attached widely to stem)

 Descending
(gills running down stem for some length)

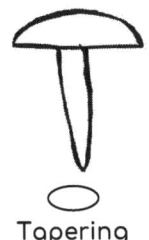 Tapering

 Equal

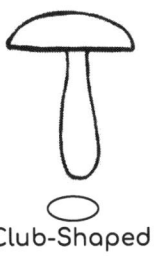 Club-Shaped

 Bulbous

 Cup (volva)

Morels

- Edible ☺
- Honeycombed cap
- Most morels cap is longer than stem
- Spore print is usually light colored
- Interior is hollow

Puffballs

- Edible ☺
- Color is white
- Rounded-shaped balls with or without spiny warts on top
- Can be mistaken for golf ball, baseball or even soccer ball

Fly Agaric

- Poisonous ☹
- Red-brown cap - irregularly lobed, like a brain
- Tube-like hollows
- Yellowish spore print
- Smooth with more wrinkles as it ages

Oyster Mushroom

- Edible ☺
- Grows on hardwood trees
- Gills descend to base
- Gills are not saw toothed or ruffled
- Spore deposit gray

Death Cap

- Poisonous ☹
- Flattened top
- White cap with brownish scales
- Gills are free and white, turning green as they mature

Jack O'Lantern

- Poisonous ☹
- Bright orange to yellowish
- Grows in clusters
- Cap convex
- Gills narrow
- Cream spore print

Lion's Mane

- Edible ☺
- Covered all over with long, spine-like hairs
- Club-shaped fruit bodies
- Common on hardwoods

Destroying Angel

- Poisonous ☹
- White stalk and gills
- White cap or white edge and yellowish, pinkish, or tan center
- Egg-shaped cap

Chicken of the Woods

- Edible ☺
- Fan-shaped and suede-like texture
- Fruitbody with yellow, round pores
- Brownish color

Chanterelle

- Edible ☺
- Shape looks like bell of a trumpet
- Bright yellow/orange
- Similar look to Jack o'Lantern

Deadly Galerina

- Poisonous ☹
- Brownish, sticky cap, yellowish to rusty gills, ring on stalk
- Edges are curved against gills
- Gills narrow, crowded

Witches' Butter

- Edible ☺
- Small, yellow, irregularly lobed, gelatinous masses
- Grows on dead deciduous wood, especially oaks

Spore Print

_____
_____
_____
_____
_____
_____

Location

Site / GPS: _____ Date: _____

○ Living Tree ○ Leaf Litter ○ Mulch ○ Dead Tree or Wood ○ Grass
○ Soil ○ Other _____

Type of Tree(s) On or Near: _____

Forest Type: ○ Deciduous ○ Coniferous ○ Tropical ○ Other _____

Weather Conditions: _____

General

Size (overall height): _____ Color: _____ Spore Color: _____

Texture: ○ Tough ○ Brittle ○ Leathery ○ Woody ○ Soft ○ Slimy
○ Spongy ○ Powdery ○ Waxy ○ Rubbery ○ Watery (Other) _____

Bruising When Touched? ○ Yes ○ No   Notes: _____

Structures: ○ Cup ○ Ring ○ Warts   _____

Cap Characteristics

Campanulate
(bell-shaped)

Conical
(triangular)

Cylindrical
(shaped like half an egg)

Convex
(outwardly rounded)

Flat
(with top of
uniform height)

Infundibuliform
(deeply, depressed,
funnel-shaped)

Depressed
(with a low
central region)

Umbonate
(with a central
bump or knob)

Surface Markings (warts, scales, slime, etc.): _____

Cap Margin: Smooth, Inrolled, Sinuous/Wavy, Other: _____

Color Changes: _____

Undercap

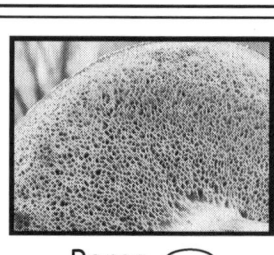

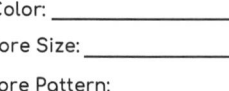

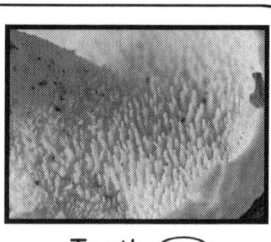

Gills ○

Attachment: Free or Decurrent

Spacing: Crowded, Close,
Distant, Subdistant

Color/Bruising: _____

Pores ○

Color: _____

Pore Size: _____

Pore Pattern: _____

Teeth ○

Color: _____

Teeth Length: _____

Flesh: Soft or Tough

◯ Free
(gills not attached to stem)

◯ Adnexed
(gills attached narrowly to stem)

◯ Sinuate
(gills smoothly notched and running briefly down stem)

◯ Adnate
(gills widely attached widely to stem)

◯ Descending
(gills running down stem for some length)

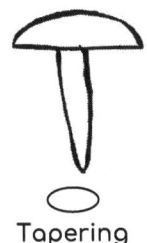  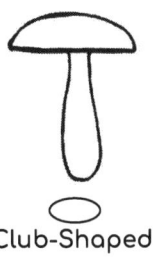 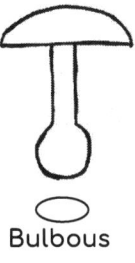  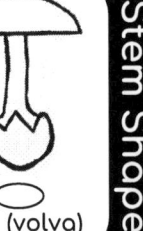

◯ Tapering

◯ Equal

◯ Club-Shaped

◯ Bulbous

◯ Cup (volva)

Morels
- Edible ☺
- Honeycombed cap
- Most morels cap is longer than stem
- Spore print is usually light colored
- Interior is hollow

Puffballs
- Edible ☺
- Color is white
- Rounded-shaped balls with or without spiny warts on top
- Can be mistaken for golf ball, baseball or even soccer ball

Fly Agaric
- Poisonous ☹
- Red-brown cap - irregularly lobed, like a brain
- Tube-like hollows
- Yellowish spore print
- Smooth with more wrinkles as it ages

Oyster Mushroom
- Edible ☺
- Grows on hardwood trees
- Gills descend to base
- Gills are not saw toothed or ruffled
- Spore deposit gray

Death Cap
- Poisonous ☹
- Flattened top
- White cap with brownish scales
- Gills are free and white, turning green as they mature

Jack O'Lantern
- Poisonous ☹
- Bright orange to yellowish
- Grows in clusters
- Cap convex
- Gills narrow
- Cream spore print

Lion's Mane
- Edible ☺
- Covered all over with long, spine-like hairs
- Club-shaped fruit bodies
- Common on hardwoods

Destroying Angel
- Poisonous ☹
- White stalk and gills
- White cap or white edge and yellowish, pinkish, or tan center
- Egg-shaped cap

Chicken of the Woods
- Edible ☺
- Fan-shaped and suede-like texture
- Fruitbody with yellow, round pores
- Brownish color

Chanterelle
- Edible ☺
- Shape looks like bell of a trumpet
- Bright yellow/orange
- Similar look to Jack o'Lantern

Deadly Galerina
- Poisonous ☹
- Brownish, sticky cap, yellowish to rusty gills, ring on stalk
- Edges are curved against gills
- Gills narrow, crowded

Witches' Butter
- Edible ☺
- Small, yellow, irregularly lobed, gelatinous masses
- Grows on dead deciduous wood, especially oaks

Spore Print

Notes

_____

_____

_____

_____

_____

_____

Location

Site / GPS: _____ Date: _____

○ Living Tree ○ Leaf Litter ○ Mulch ○ Dead Tree or Wood ○ Grass
○ Soil ○ Other _____

Type of Tree(s) On or Near: _____

Forest Type: ○ Deciduous ○ Coniferous ○ Tropical ○ Other _____

Weather Conditions: _____

General

Size (overall height): _____ Color: _____ Spore Color: _____

Texture: ○ Tough ○ Brittle ○ Leathery ○ Woody ○ Soft ○ Slimy
○ Spongy ○ Powdery ○ Waxy ○ Rubbery ○ Watery (Other) _____

Bruising When Touched? ○ Yes ○ No   Notes: _____

Structures: ○ Cup ○ Ring ○ Warts   _____

Cap Characteristics

Campanulate
(bell-shaped)

Conical
(triangular)

Cylindrical
(shaped like half an egg)

Convex
(outwardly rounded)

Flat
(with top of uniform height)

Infundibuliform
(deeply, depressed, funnel-shaped)

Depressed
(with a low central region)

Umbonate
(with a central bump or knob)

Surface Markings (warts, scales, slime, etc.): _____

Cap Margin: Smooth, Inrolled, Sinuous/Wavy, Other:_____

Color Changes: _____

Undercap

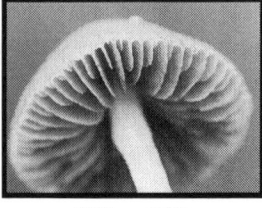

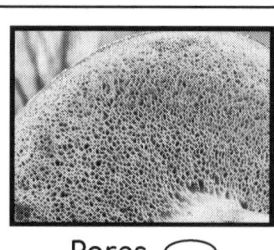

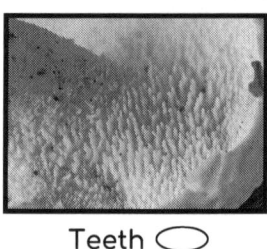

Gills ○
Attachment: Free or Decurrent
Spacing: Crowded, Close,
          Distant, Subdistant
Color/Bruising: _____

Pores ○
Color: _____
Pore Size: _____
Pore Pattern: _____

Teeth ○
Color: _____
Teeth Length: _____
Flesh: Soft or Tough

Free
(gills not attached to stem)

Adnexed
(gills attached narrowly to stem)

Sinuate
(gills smoothly notched and running briefly down stem)

Adnate
(gills widely attached widely to stem)

Descending
(gills running down stem for some length)

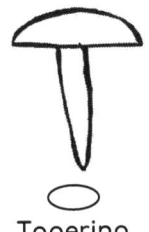

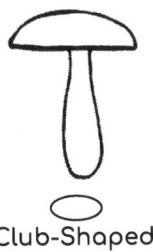
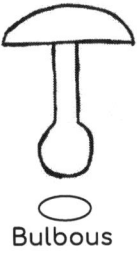
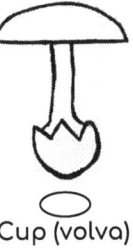

Tapering

Equal

Club-Shaped

Bulbous

Cup (volva)

Morels

- Edible ☺
- Honeycombed cap
- Most morels cap is longer than stem
- Spore print is usually light colored
- Interior is hollow

Puffballs

- Edible ☺
- Color is white
- Rounded-shaped balls with or without spiny warts on top
- Can be mistaken for golf ball, baseball or even soccer ball

Fly Agaric

- Poisonous ☹
- Red-brown cap - irregularly lobed, like a brain
- Tube-like hollows
- Yellowish spore print
- Smooth with more wrinkles as it ages

Oyster Mushroom

- Edible ☺
- Grows on hardwood trees
- Gills descend to base
- Gills are not saw toothed or ruffled
- Spore deposit gray

Death Cap

- Poisonous ☹
- Flattened top
- White cap with brownish scales
- Gills are free and white, turning green as they mature

Jack O'Lantern

- Poisonous ☹
- Bright orange to yellowish
- Grows in clusters
- Cap convex
- Gills narrow
- Cream spore print

Lion's Mane

- Edible ☺
- Covered all over with long, spine-like hairs
- Club-shaped fruit bodies
- Common on hardwoods

Destroying Angel

- Poisonous ☹
- White stalk and gills
- White cap or white edge and yellowish, pinkish, or tan center
- Egg-shaped cap

Chicken of the Woods

- Edible ☺
- Fan-shaped and suede-like texture
- Fruitbody with yellow, round pores
- Brownish color

Chanterelle

- Edible ☺
- Shape looks like bell of a trumpet
- Bright yellow/orange
- Similar look to Jack o'Lantern

Deadly Galerina

- Poisonous ☹
- Brownish, sticky cap, yellowish to rusty gills, ring on stalk
- Edges are curved against gills
- Gills narrow, crowded

Witches' Butter

- Edible ☺
- Small, yellow, irregularly lobed, gelatinous masses
- Grows on dead deciduous wood, especially oaks

Spore Print

Location

Site / GPS: _____ Date: _____

○ Living Tree   ○ Leaf Litter   ○ Mulch   ○ Dead Tree or Wood   ○ Grass
○ Soil   ○ Other _____

Type of Tree(s) On or Near: _____

Forest Type: ○ Deciduous   ○ Coniferous   ○ Tropical   ○ Other _____

Weather Conditions: _____

General

Size (overall height): _____   Color: _____   Spore Color: _____

Texture: ○ Tough   ○ Brittle   ○ Leathery   ○ Woody   ○ Soft   ○ Slimy
○ Spongy   ○ Powdery   ○ Waxy   ○ Rubbery   ○ Watery   (Other) _____

Bruising When Touched? ○ Yes   ○ No   Notes: _____

Structures: ○ Cup   ○ Ring   ○ Warts   _____

Cap Characteristics

Campanulate
(bell-shaped)

Conical
(triangular)

Cylindrical
(shaped like half an egg)

Convex
(outwardly rounded)

Flat
(with top of
uniform height)

Infundibuliform
(deeply, depressed,
funnel-shaped)

Depressed
(with a low
central region)

Umbonate
(with a central
bump or knob)

Surface Markings (warts, scales, slime, etc.): _____

Cap Margin: Smooth, Inrolled, Sinuous/Wavy, Other: _____

Color Changes: _____

Undercap

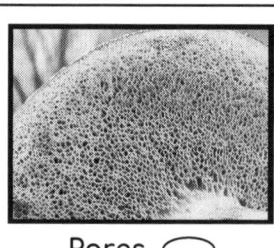

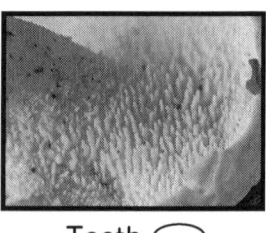

Gills ○
Attachment: Free or Decurrent
Spacing: Crowded, Close,
Distant, Subdistant
Color/Bruising: _____

Pores ○
Color: _____
Pore Size: _____
Pore Pattern: _____

Teeth ○
Color: _____
Teeth Length: _____
Flesh: Soft or Tough

○ Free
(gills not attached to stem)

○ Adnexed
(gills attached narrowly to stem)

○ Sinuate
(gills smoothly notched and running briefly down stem)

○ Adnate
(gills widely attached widely to stem)

○ Descending
(gills running down stem for some length)

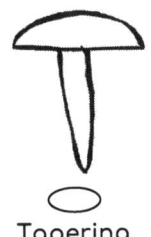  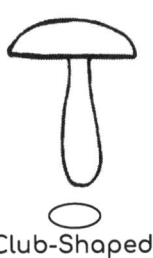 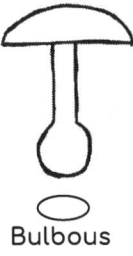 

○ Tapering   ○ Equal   ○ Club-Shaped   ○ Bulbous   ○ Cup (volva)

Morels
- Edible ☺
- Honeycombed cap
- Most morels cap is longer than stem
- Spore print is usually light colored
- Interior is hollow

Puffballs
- Edible ☺
- Color is white
- Rounded-shaped balls with or without spiny warts on top
- Can be mistaken for golf ball, baseball or even soccer ball

Fly Agaric
- Poisonous ☹
- Red-brown cap - irregularly lobed, like a brain
- Tube-like hollows
- Yellowish spore print
- Smooth with more wrinkles as it ages

Oyster Mushroom
- Edible ☺
- Grows on hardwood trees
- Gills descend to base
- Gills are not saw toothed or ruffled
- Spore deposit gray

Death Cap
- Poisonous ☹
- Flattened top
- White cap with brownish scales
- Gills are free and white, turning green as they mature

Jack O'Lantern
- Poisonous ☹
- Bright orange to yellowish
- Grows in clusters
- Cap convex
- Gills narrow
- Cream spore print

Lion's Mane
- Edible ☺
- Covered all over with long, spine-like hairs
- Club-shaped fruit bodies
- Common on hardwoods

Destroying Angel
- Poisonous ☹
- White stalk and gills
- White cap or white edge and yellowish, pinkish, or tan center
- Egg-shaped cap

Chicken of the Woods
- Edible ☺
- Fan-shaped and suede-like texture
- Fruitbody with yellow, round pores
- Brownish color

Chanterelle
- Edible ☺
- Shape looks like bell of a trumpet
- Bright yellow/orange
- Similar look to Jack o'Lantern

Deadly Galerina
- Poisonous ☹
- Brownish, sticky cap, yellowish to rusty gills, ring on stalk
- Edges are curved against gills
- Gills narrow, crowded

Witches' Butter
- Edible ☺
- Small, yellow, irregularly lobed, gelatinous masses
- Grows on dead deciduous wood, especially oaks

Spore Print

_____
_____
_____
_____
_____
_____

Location

Site / GPS: _____ Date: _____

⬭ Living Tree ⬭ Leaf Litter ⬭ Mulch ⬭ Dead Tree or Wood ⬭ Grass

⬭ Soil ⬭ Other _____

Type of Tree(s) On or Near: _____

Forest Type: ⬭ Deciduous ⬭ Coniferous ⬭ Tropical ⬭ Other _____

Weather Conditions: _____

General

Size (overall height): _____ Color: _____ Spore Color: _____

Texture: ⬭ Tough ⬭ Brittle ⬭ Leathery ⬭ Woody ⬭ Soft ⬭ Slimy

⬭ Spongy ⬭ Powdery ⬭ Waxy ⬭ Rubbery ⬭ Watery (Other) _____

Bruising When Touched? ⬭ Yes ⬭ No   Notes: _____

Structures: ⬭ Cup ⬭ Ring ⬭ Warts   _____

Cap Characteristics

Campanulate
(bell-shaped)

Conical
(triangular)

Cylindrical
(shaped like half an egg)

Convex
(outwardly rounded)

Flat
(with top of uniform height)

Infundibuliform
(deeply, depressed, funnel-shaped)

Depressed
(with a low central region)

Umbonate
(with a central bump or knob)

Surface Markings (warts, scales, slime, etc.): _____

Cap Margin: Smooth, Inrolled, Sinuous/Wavy, Other:_____

Color Changes: _____

Undercap

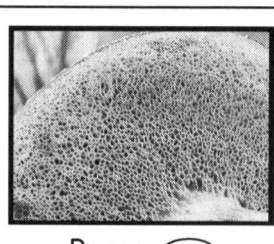

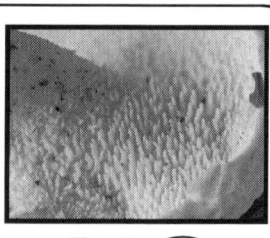

Gills ⬭
Attachment: Free or Decurrent

Spacing: Crowded, Close, Distant, Subdistant

Color/Bruising: _____

Pores ⬭
Color: _____

Pore Size: _____

Pore Pattern: _____

Teeth ⬭
Color: _____

Teeth Length: _____

Flesh: Soft or Tough

○ Free
(gills not attached to stem)

○ Adnexed
(gills attached narrowly to stem)

○ Sinuate
(gills smoothly notched and running briefly down stem)

○ Adnate
(gills widely attached widely to stem)

○ Descending
(gills running down stem for some length)

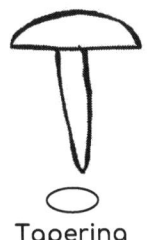  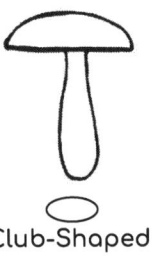 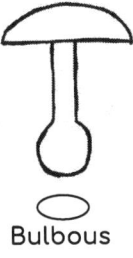 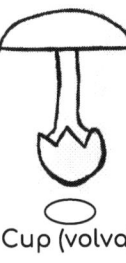 

○ Tapering

○ Equal

○ Club-Shaped

○ Bulbous

○ Cup (volva)

Morels
- Edible ☺
- Honeycombed cap
- Most morels cap is longer than stem
- Spore print is usually light colored
- Interior is hollow

Puffballs
- Edible ☺
- Color is white
- Rounded-shaped balls with or without spiny warts on top
- Can be mistaken for golf ball, baseball or even soccer ball

Fly Agaric
- Poisonous ☹
- Red-brown cap - irregularly lobed, like a brain
- Tube-like hollows
- Yellowish spore print
- Smooth with more wrinkles as it ages

Oyster Mushroom
- Edible ☺
- Grows on hardwood trees
- Gills descend to base
- Gills are not saw toothed or ruffled
- Spore deposit gray

Death Cap
- Poisonous ☹
- Flattened top
- White cap with brownish scales
- Gills are free and white, turning green as they mature

Jack O'Lantern
- Poisonous ☹
- Bright orange to yellowish
- Grows in clusters
- Cap convex
- Gills narrow
- Cream spore print

Lion's Mane
- Edible ☺
- Covered all over with long, spine-like hairs
- Club-shaped fruit bodies
- Common on hardwoods

Destroying Angel
- Poisonous ☹
- White stalk and gills
- White cap or white edge and yellowish, pinkish, or tan center
- Egg-shaped cap

Chicken of the Woods
- Edible ☺
- Fan-shaped and suede-like texture
- Fruitbody with yellow, round pores
- Brownish color

Chanterelle
- Edible ☺
- Shape looks like bell of a trumpet
- Bright yellow/orange
- Similar look to Jack o'Lantern

Deadly Galerina
- Poisonous ☹
- Brownish, sticky cap, yellowish to rusty gills, ring on stalk
- Edges are curved against gills
- Gills narrow, crowded

Witches' Butter
- Edible ☺
- Small, yellow, irregularly lobed, gelatinous masses
- Grows on dead deciduous wood, especially oaks

Spore Print

_____
_____
_____
_____
_____
_____

Location

Site / GPS: _____ Date: _____

○ Living Tree ○ Leaf Litter ○ Mulch ○ Dead Tree or Wood ○ Grass
○ Soil ○ Other _____

Type of Tree(s) On or Near: _____

Forest Type: ○ Deciduous ○ Coniferous ○ Tropical ○ Other _____

Weather Conditions: _____

General

Size (overall height): _____ Color: _____ Spore Color: _____

Texture: ○ Tough ○ Brittle ○ Leathery ○ Woody ○ Soft ○ Slimy
○ Spongy ○ Powdery ○ Waxy ○ Rubbery ○ Watery (Other) _____

Bruising When Touched? ○ Yes ○ No Notes: _____

Structures: ○ Cup ○ Ring ○ Warts _____

Cap Characteristics

Campanulate
(bell-shaped)

Conical
(triangular)

Cylindrical
(shaped like half an egg)

Convex
(outwardly rounded)

Flat
(with top of
uniform height)

Infundibuliform
(deeply, depressed,
funnel-shaped)

Depressed
(with a low
central region)

Umbonate
(with a central
bump or knob)

Surface Markings (warts, scales, slime, etc.): _____

Cap Margin: Smooth, Inrolled, Sinuous/Wavy, Other:_____

Color Changes: _____

Undercap

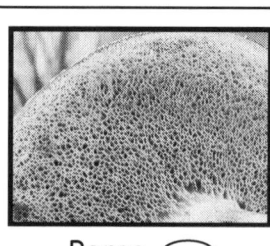

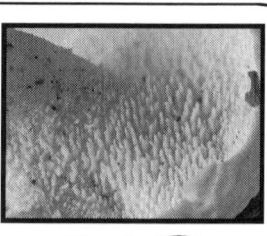

Gills ○

Attachment: Free or Decurrent

Spacing: Crowded, Close,
         Distant, Subdistant

Color/Bruising: _____

Pores ○

Color: _____

Pore Size: _____

Pore Pattern: _____

Teeth ○

Color: _____

Teeth Length: _____

Flesh: Soft or Tough

Free	Adnexed	Sinuate	Adnate	Descending
(gills not attached to stem)	(gills attached narrowly to stem)	(gills smoothly notched and running briefly down stem)	(gills widely attached widely to stem)	(gills running down stem for some length)

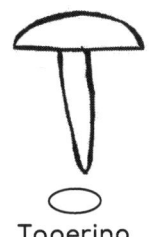  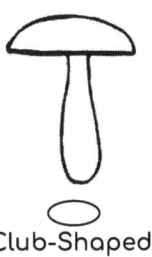 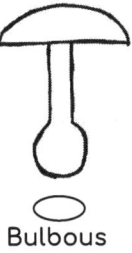 

Tapering	Equal	Club-Shaped	Bulbous	Cup (volva)

Morels

- Edible ☺
- Honeycombed cap
- Most morels cap is longer than stem
- Spore print is usually light colored
- Interior is hollow

Puffballs

- Edible ☺
- Color is white
- Rounded-shaped balls with or without spiny warts on top
- Can be mistaken for golf ball, baseball or even soccer ball

Fly Agaric

- Poisonous ☹
- Red-brown cap - irregularly lobed, like a brain
- Tube-like hollows
- Yellowish spore print
- Smooth with more wrinkles as it ages

Oyster Mushroom

- Edible ☺
- Grows on hardwood trees
- Gills descend to base
- Gills are not saw toothed or ruffled
- Spore deposit gray

Death Cap

- Poisonous ☹
- Flattened top
- White cap with brownish scales
- Gills are free and white, turning green as they mature

Jack O'Lantern

- Poisonous ☹
- Bright orange to yellowish
- Grows in clusters
- Cap convex
- Gills narrow
- Cream spore print

Lion's Mane

- Edible ☺
- Covered all over with long, spine-like hairs
- Club-shaped fruit bodies
- Common on hardwoods

Destroying Angel

- Poisonous ☹
- White stalk and gills
- White cap or white edge and yellowish, pinkish, or tan center
- Egg-shaped cap

Chicken of the Woods

- Edible ☺
- Fan-shaped and suede-like texture
- Fruitbody with yellow, round pores
- Brownish color

Chanterelle

- Edible ☺
- Shape looks like bell of a trumpet
- Bright yellow/orange
- Similar look to Jack o'Lantern

Deadly Galerina

- Poisonous ☹
- Brownish, sticky cap, yellowish to rusty gills, ring on stalk
- Edges are curved against gills
- Gills narrow, crowded

Witches' Butter

- Edible ☺
- Small, yellow, irregularly lobed, gelatinous masses
- Grows on dead deciduous wood, especially oaks

Spore Print

_____
_____
_____
_____
_____
_____

Location

Site / GPS: _____ Date: _____

○ Living Tree ○ Leaf Litter ○ Mulch ○ Dead Tree or Wood ○ Grass
○ Soil ○ Other _____

Type of Tree(s) On or Near: _____

Forest Type: ○ Deciduous ○ Coniferous ○ Tropical ○ Other _____

Weather Conditions: _____

General

Size (overall height): _____ Color: _____ Spore Color: _____

Texture: ○ Tough ○ Brittle ○ Leathery ○ Woody ○ Soft ○ Slimy
○ Spongy ○ Powdery ○ Waxy ○ Rubbery ○ Watery (Other) _____

Bruising When Touched? ○ Yes ○ No   Notes: _____

Structures: ○ Cup ○ Ring ○ Warts   _____

Cap Characteristics

Campanulate
(bell-shaped)

Conical
(triangular)

Cylindrical
(shaped like half an egg)

Convex
(outwardly rounded)

Flat
(with top of
uniform height)

Infundibuliform
(deeply, depressed,
funnel-shaped)

Depressed
(with a low
central region)

Umbonate
(with a central
bump or knob)

Surface Markings (warts, scales, slime, etc.): _____

Cap Margin: Smooth, Inrolled, Sinuous/Wavy, Other: _____

Color Changes: _____

Undercap

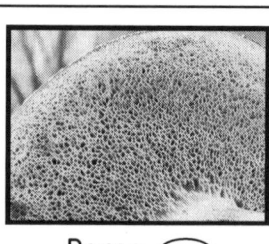

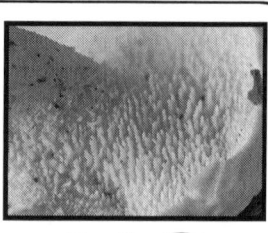

Gills ○

Attachment: Free or Decurrent

Spacing: Crowded, Close,
Distant, Subdistant

Color/Bruising: _____

Pores ○

Color: _____

Pore Size: _____

Pore Pattern: _____

Teeth ○

Color: _____

Teeth Length: _____

Flesh: Soft or Tough

- ⬭ **Free**
  (gills not attached to stem)
- ⬭ **Adnexed**
  (gills attached narrowly to stem)
- ⬭ **Sinuate**
  (gills smoothly notched and running briefly down stem)
- ⬭ **Adnate**
  (gills widely attached widely to stem)
- ⬭ **Descending**
  (gills running down stem for some length)

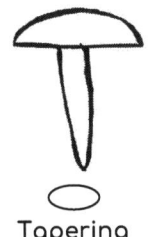  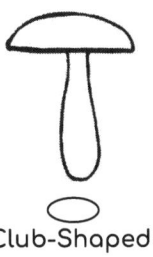 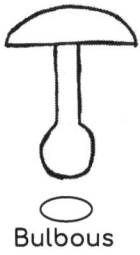  

- ⬭ **Tapering**
- ⬭ **Equal**
- ⬭ **Club-Shaped**
- ⬭ **Bulbous**
- ⬭ **Cup (volva)**

Morels
- Edible ☺
- Honeycombed cap
- Most morels cap is longer than stem
- Spore print is usually light colored
- Interior is hollow

Puffballs
- Edible ☺
- Color is white
- Rounded-shaped balls with or without spiny warts on top
- Can be mistaken for golf ball, baseball or even soccer ball

Fly Agaric
- Poisonous ☹
- Red-brown cap - irregularly lobed, like a brain
- Tube-like hollows
- Yellowish spore print
- Smooth with more wrinkles as it ages

Oyster Mushroom
- Edible ☺
- Grows on hardwood trees
- Gills descend to base
- Gills are not saw toothed or ruffled
- Spore deposit gray

Death Cap
- Poisonous ☹
- Flattened top
- White cap with brownish scales
- Gills are free and white, turning green as they mature

Jack O'Lantern
- Poisonous ☹
- Bright orange to yellowish
- Grows in clusters
- Cap convex
- Gills narrow
- Cream spore print

Lion's Mane
- Edible ☺
- Covered all over with long, spine-like hairs
- Club-shaped fruit bodies
- Common on hardwoods

Destroying Angel
- Poisonous ☹
- White stalk and gills
- White cap or white edge and yellowish, pinkish, or tan center
- Egg-shaped cap

Chicken of the Woods
- Edible ☺
- Fan-shaped and suede-like texture
- Fruitbody with yellow, round pores
- Brownish color

Chanterelle
- Edible ☺
- Shape looks like bell of a trumpet
- Bright yellow/orange
- Similar look to Jack o'Lantern

Deadly Galerina
- Poisonous ☹
- Brownish, sticky cap, yellowish to rusty gills, ring on stalk
- Edges are curved against gills
- Gills narrow, crowded

Witches' Butter
- Edible ☺
- Small, yellow, irregularly lobed, gelatinous masses
- Grows on dead deciduous wood, especially oaks

Spore Print

_____
_____
_____
_____
_____
_____

Location

Site / GPS: _____ Date: _____

○ Living Tree ○ Leaf Litter ○ Mulch ○ Dead Tree or Wood ○ Grass
○ Soil ○ Other _____

Type of Tree(s) On or Near: _____

Forest Type: ○ Deciduous ○ Coniferous ○ Tropical ○ Other _____

Weather Conditions: _____

General

Size (overall height): _____ Color: _____ Spore Color: _____

Texture: ○ Tough ○ Brittle ○ Leathery ○ Woody ○ Soft ○ Slimy
○ Spongy ○ Powdery ○ Waxy ○ Rubbery ○ Watery (Other) _____

Bruising When Touched? ○ Yes ○ No   Notes: _____

Structures: ○ Cup ○ Ring ○ Warts   _____

Cap Characteristics

Campanulate
(bell-shaped)

Conical
(triangular)

Cylindrical
(shaped like half an egg)

Convex
(outwardly rounded)

Flat
(with top of uniform height)

Infundibuliform
(deeply, depressed, funnel-shaped)

Depressed
(with a low central region)

Umbonate
(with a central bump or knob)

Surface Markings (warts, scales, slime, etc.): _____

Cap Margin: Smooth, Inrolled, Sinuous/Wavy, Other: _____

Color Changes: _____

Undercap

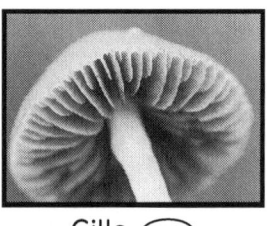

Gills ○

Attachment: Free or Decurrent

Spacing: Crowded, Close, Distant, Subdistant

Color/Bruising: _____

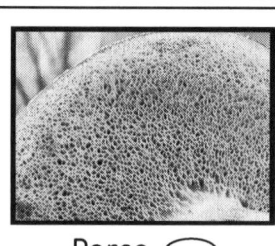

Pores ○

Color: _____

Pore Size: _____

Pore Pattern: _____

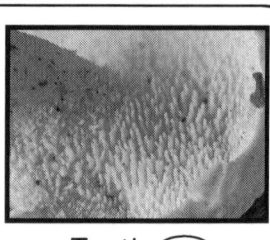

Teeth ○

Color: _____

Teeth Length: _____

Flesh: Soft or Tough

Free	Adnexed	Sinuate	Adnate	Descending
(gills not attached to stem)	(gills attached narrowly to stem)	(gills smoothly notched and running briefly down stem)	(gills widely attached widely to stem)	(gills running down stem for some length)

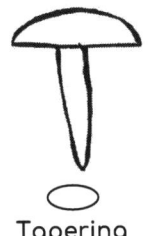  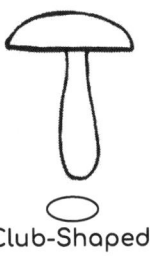 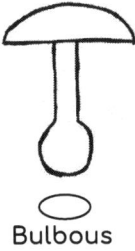 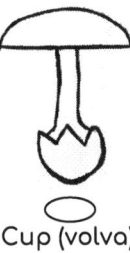

| Tapering | Equal | Club-Shaped | Bulbous | Cup (volva) |

Morels
- Edible ☺
- Honeycombed cap
- Most morels cap is longer than stem
- Spore print is usually light colored
- Interior is hollow

Puffballs
- Edible ☺
- Color is white
- Rounded-shaped balls with or without spiny warts on top
- Can be mistaken for golf ball, baseball or even soccer ball

Fly Agaric
- Poisonous ☹
- Red-brown cap - irregularly lobed, like a brain
- Tube-like hollows
- Yellowish spore print
- Smooth with more wrinkles as it ages

Oyster Mushroom
- Edible ☺
- Grows on hardwood trees
- Gills descend to base
- Gills are not saw toothed or ruffled
- Spore deposit gray

Death Cap
- Poisonous ☹
- Flattened top
- White cap with brownish scales
- Gills are free and white, turning green as they mature

Jack O'Lantern
- Poisonous ☹
- Bright orange to yellowish
- Grows in clusters
- Cap convex
- Gills narrow
- Cream spore print

Lion's Mane
- Edible ☺
- Covered all over with long, spine-like hairs
- Club-shaped fruit bodies
- Common on hardwoods

Destroying Angel
- Poisonous ☹
- White stalk and gills
- White cap or white edge and yellowish, pinkish, or tan center
- Egg-shaped cap

Chicken of the Woods
- Edible ☺
- Fan-shaped and suede-like texture
- Fruitbody with yellow, round pores
- Brownish color

Chanterelle
- Edible ☺
- Shape looks like bell of a trumpet
- Bright yellow/orange
- Similar look to Jack o'Lantern

Deadly Galerina
- Poisonous ☹
- Brownish, sticky cap, yellowish to rusty gills, ring on stalk
- Edges are curved against gills
- Gills narrow, crowded

Witches' Butter
- Edible ☺
- Small, yellow, irregularly lobed, gelatinous masses
- Grows on dead deciduous wood, especially oaks

Spore Print

_____
_____
_____
_____
_____
_____

Location

Site / GPS: _____ Date: _____

◯ Living Tree ◯ Leaf Litter ◯ Mulch ◯ Dead Tree or Wood ◯ Grass
◯ Soil ◯ Other _____

Type of Tree(s) On or Near: _____

Forest Type: ◯ Deciduous ◯ Coniferous ◯ Tropical ◯ Other _____

Weather Conditions: _____

General

Size (overall height): _____ Color: _____ Spore Color: _____

Texture: ◯ Tough ◯ Brittle ◯ Leathery ◯ Woody ◯ Soft ◯ Slimy
◯ Spongy ◯ Powdery ◯ Waxy ◯ Rubbery ◯ Watery (Other) _____

Bruising When Touched? ◯ Yes ◯ No   Notes: _____

Structures: ◯ Cup ◯ Ring ◯ Warts   _____

Cap Characteristics

Campanulate
(bell-shaped)

Conical
(triangular)

Cylindrical
(shaped like half an egg)

Convex
(outwardly rounded)

Flat
(with top of
uniform height)

Infundibuliform
(deeply, depressed,
funnel-shaped)

Depressed
(with a low
central region)

Umbonate
(with a central
bump or knob)

Surface Markings (warts, scales, slime, etc.): _____

Cap Margin: Smooth, Inrolled, Sinuous/Wavy, Other: _____

Color Changes: _____

Undercap

Gills ◯

Attachment: Free or Decurrent

Spacing: Crowded, Close,
Distant, Subdistant

Color/Bruising: _____

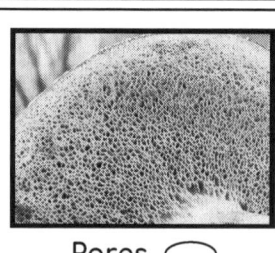

Pores ◯

Color: _____

Pore Size: _____

Pore Pattern: _____

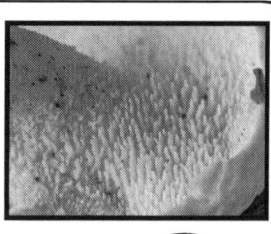

Teeth ◯

Color: _____

Teeth Length: _____

Flesh: Soft or Tough

○ Free
(gills not attached to stem)

○ Adnexed
(gills attached narrowly to stem)

○ Sinuate
(gills smoothly notched and running briefly down stem)

○ Adnate
(gills widely attached widely to stem)

○ Descending
(gills running down stem for some length)

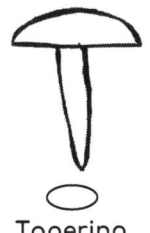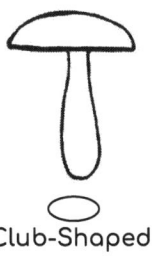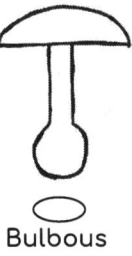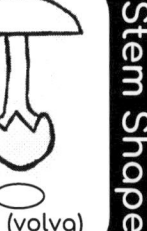

Tapering   Equal   Club-Shaped   Bulbous   Cup (volva)

Morels
- Edible ☺
- Honeycombed cap
- Most morels cap is longer than stem
- Spore print is usually light colored
- Interior is hollow

Puffballs
- Edible ☺
- Color is white
- Rounded-shaped balls with or without spiny warts on top
- Can be mistaken for golf ball, baseball or even soccer ball

Fly Agaric
- Poisonous ☹
- Red-brown cap - irregularly lobed, like a brain
- Tube-like hollows
- Yellowish spore print
- Smooth with more wrinkles as it ages

Oyster Mushroom
- Edible ☺
- Grows on hardwood trees
- Gills descend to base
- Gills are not saw toothed or ruffled
- Spore deposit gray

Death Cap
- Poisonous ☹
- Flattened top
- White cap with brownish scales
- Gills are free and white, turning green as they mature

Jack O'Lantern
- Poisonous ☹
- Bright orange to yellowish
- Grows in clusters
- Cap convex
- Gills narrow
- Cream spore print

Lion's Mane
- Edible ☺
- Covered all over with long, spine-like hairs
- Club-shaped fruit bodies
- Common on hardwoods

Destroying Angel
- Poisonous ☹
- White stalk and gills
- White cap or white edge and yellowish, pinkish, or tan center
- Egg-shaped cap

Chicken of the Woods
- Edible ☺
- Fan-shaped and suede-like texture
- Fruitbody with yellow, round pores
- Brownish color

Chanterelle
- Edible ☺
- Shape looks like bell of a trumpet
- Bright yellow/orange
- Similar look to Jack o'Lantern

Deadly Galerina
- Poisonous ☹
- Brownish, sticky cap, yellowish to rusty gills, ring on stalk
- Edges are curved against gills
- Gills narrow, crowded

Witches' Butter
- Edible ☺
- Small, yellow, irregularly lobed, gelatinous masses
- Grows on dead deciduous wood, especially oaks

Spore Print

Location

Site / GPS: _____ Date: _____

○ Living Tree ○ Leaf Litter ○ Mulch ○ Dead Tree or Wood ○ Grass
○ Soil ○ Other _____

Type of Tree(s) On or Near: _____

Forest Type: ○ Deciduous ○ Coniferous ○ Tropical ○ Other _____

Weather Conditions: _____

General

Size (overall height): _____ Color: _____ Spore Color: _____

Texture: ○ Tough ○ Brittle ○ Leathery ○ Woody ○ Soft ○ Slimy
○ Spongy ○ Powdery ○ Waxy ○ Rubbery ○ Watery (Other) _____

Bruising When Touched? ○ Yes ○ No   Notes: _____

Structures: ○ Cup ○ Ring ○ Warts   _____

Cap Characteristics

Campanulate
(bell-shaped)

Conical
(triangular)

Cylindrical
(shaped like half an egg)

Convex
(outwardly rounded)

Flat
(with top of
uniform height)

Infundibuliform
(deeply, depressed,
funnel-shaped)

Depressed
(with a low
central region)

Umbonate
(with a central
bump or knob)

Surface Markings (warts, scales, slime, etc.): _____

Cap Margin: Smooth, Inrolled, Sinuous/Wavy, Other: _____

Color Changes: _____

Undercap

Gills ○

Attachment: Free or Decurrent

Spacing: Crowded, Close,
            Distant, Subdistant

Color/Bruising: _____

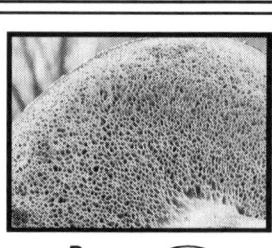

Pores ○

Color: _____

Pore Size: _____

Pore Pattern: _____

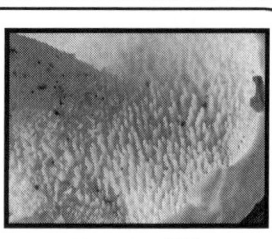

Teeth ○

Color: _____

Teeth Length: _____

Flesh: Soft or Tough

○ **Free**
(gills not attached to stem)

 ○ **Adnexed**
(gills attached narrowly to stem)

 ○ **Sinuate**
(gills smoothly notched and running briefly down stem)

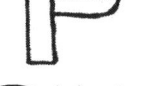 ○ **Adnate**
(gills widely attached widely to stem)

 ○ **Descenting**
(gills running down stem for some length)

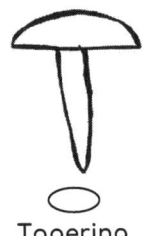 **Tapering** ○

 **Equal** ○

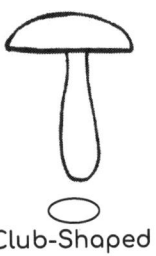 **Club-Shaped** ○

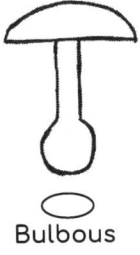 **Bulbous** ○

 **Cup (volva)** ○

Morels
- Edible ☺
- Honeycombed cap
- Most morels cap is longer than stem
- Spore print is usually light colored
- Interior is hollow

Puffballs
- Edible ☺
- Color is white
- Rounded-shaped balls with or without spiny warts on top
- Can be mistaken for golf ball, baseball or even soccer ball

Fly Agaric
- Poisonous ☹
- Red-brown cap - irregularly lobed, like a brain
- Tube-like hollows
- Yellowish spore print
- Smooth with more wrinkles as it ages

Oyster Mushroom
- Edible ☺
- Grows on hardwood trees
- Gills descend to base
- Gills are not saw toothed or ruffled
- Spore deposit gray

Death Cap
- Poisonous ☹
- Flattened top
- White cap with brownish scales
- Gills are free and white, turning green as they mature

Jack O'Lantern
- Poisonous ☹
- Bright orange to yellowish
- Grows in clusters
- Cap convex
- Gills narrow
- Cream spore print

Lion's Mane
- Edible ☺
- Covered all over with long, spine-like hairs
- Club-shaped fruit bodies
- Common on hardwoods

Destroying Angel
- Poisonous ☹
- White stalk and gills
- White cap or white edge and yellowish, pinkish, or tan center
- Egg-shaped cap

Chicken of the Woods
- Edible ☺
- Fan-shaped and suede-like texture
- Fruitbody with yellow, round pores
- Brownish color

Chanterelle
- Edible ☺
- Shape looks like bell of a trumpet
- Bright yellow/orange
- Similar look to Jack o'Lantern

Deadly Galerina
- Poisonous ☹
- Brownish, sticky cap, yellowish to rusty gills, ring on stalk
- Edges are curved against gills
- Gills narrow, crowded

Witches' Butter
- Edible ☺
- Small, yellow, irregularly lobed, gelatinous masses
- Grows on dead deciduous wood, especially oaks

Spore Print

_____

_____

_____

_____

_____

Location

Site / GPS: _____ Date: _____

◯ Living Tree ◯ Leaf Litter ◯ Mulch ◯ Dead Tree or Wood ◯ Grass
◯ Soil ◯ Other _____

Type of Tree(s) On or Near: _____

Forest Type: ◯ Deciduous ◯ Coniferous ◯ Tropical ◯ Other _____

Weather Conditions: _____

General

Size (overall height): _____ Color: _____ Spore Color: _____

Texture: ◯ Tough ◯ Brittle ◯ Leathery ◯ Woody ◯ Soft ◯ Slimy
◯ Spongy ◯ Powdery ◯ Waxy ◯ Rubbery ◯ Watery (Other) _____

Bruising When Touched? ◯ Yes ◯ No   Notes: _____

Structures: ◯ Cup ◯ Ring ◯ Warts   _____

Cap Characteristics

Campanulate
(bell-shaped)

Conical
(triangular)

Cylindrical
(shaped like half an egg)

Convex
(outwardly rounded)

Flat
(with top of
uniform height)

Infundibuliform
(deeply, depressed,
funnel-shaped)

Depressed
(with a low
central region)

Umbonate
(with a central
bump or knob)

Surface Markings (warts, scales, slime, etc.): _____

Cap Margin: Smooth, Inrolled, Sinuous/Wavy, Other: _____

Color Changes: _____

Undercap

Gills ◯

Attachment: Free or Decurrent

Spacing: Crowded, Close,
         Distant, Subdistant

Color/Bruising: _____

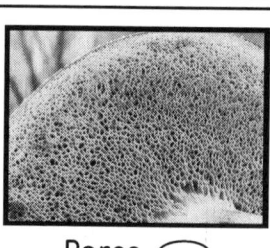

Pores ◯

Color: _____

Pore Size: _____

Pore Pattern: _____

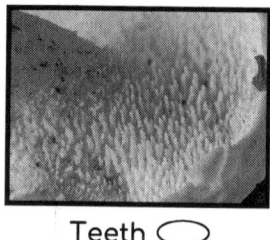

Teeth ◯

Color: _____

Teeth Length: _____

Flesh: Soft or Tough

◯ Free	◯ Adnexed	◯ Sinuate	◯ Adnate	◯ Descending
(gills not attached to stem)	(gills attached narrowly to stem)	(gills smoothly notched and running briefly down stem)	(gills widely attached widely to stem)	(gills running down stem for some length)

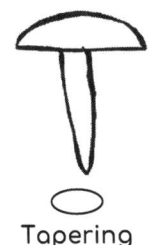  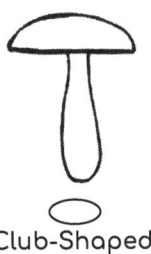 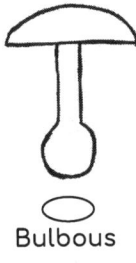 

Tapering	Equal	Club-Shaped	Bulbous	Cup (volva)

Morels
- Edible ☺
- Honeycombed cap
- Most morels cap is longer than stem
- Spore print is usually light colored
- Interior is hollow

Puffballs
- Edible ☺
- Color is white
- Rounded-shaped balls with or without spiny warts on top
- Can be mistaken for golf ball, baseball or even soccer ball

Fly Agaric
- Poisonous ☹
- Red-brown cap - irregularly lobed, like a brain
- Tube-like hollows
- Yellowish spore print
- Smooth with more wrinkles as it ages

Oyster Mushroom
- Edible ☺
- Grows on hardwood trees
- Gills descend to base
- Gills are not saw toothed or ruffled
- Spore deposit gray

Death Cap
- Poisonous ☹
- Flattened top
- White cap with brownish scales
- Gills are free and white, turning green as they mature

Jack O'Lantern
- Poisonous ☹
- Bright orange to yellowish
- Grows in clusters
- Cap convex
- Gills narrow
- Cream spore print

Lion's Mane
- Edible ☺
- Covered all over with long, spine-like hairs
- Club-shaped fruit bodies
- Common on hardwoods

Destroying Angel
- Poisonous ☹
- White stalk and gills
- White cap or white edge and yellowish, pinkish, or tan center
- Egg-shaped cap

Chicken of the Woods
- Edible ☺
- Fan-shaped and suede-like texture
- Fruitbody with yellow, round pores
- Brownish color

Chanterelle
- Edible ☺
- Shape looks like bell of a trumpet
- Bright yellow/orange
- Similar look to Jack o'Lantern

Deadly Galerina
- Poisonous ☹
- Brownish, sticky cap, yellowish to rusty gills, ring on stalk
- Edges are curved against gills
- Gills narrow, crowded

Witches' Butter
- Edible ☺
- Small, yellow, irregularly lobed, gelatinous masses
- Grows on dead deciduous wood, especially oaks

Spore Print

_____

_____

_____

_____

_____

_____

Location

Site / GPS: _____ Date: _____

○ Living Tree   ○ Leaf Litter   ○ Mulch   ○ Dead Tree or Wood   ○ Grass

○ Soil   ○ Other _____

Type of Tree(s) On or Near: _____

Forest Type: ○ Deciduous   ○ Coniferous   ○ Tropical   ○ Other _____

Weather Conditions: _____

General

Size (overall height): _____   Color: _____   Spore Color: _____

Texture: ○ Tough   ○ Brittle   ○ Leathery   ○ Woody   ○ Soft   ○ Slimy

○ Spongy   ○ Powdery   ○ Waxy   ○ Rubbery   ○ Watery   (Other) _____

Bruising When Touched? ○ Yes   ○ No   Notes: _____

Structures: ○ Cup   ○ Ring   ○ Warts   _____

Cap Characteristics

Campanulate
(bell-shaped)

Conical
(triangular)

Cylindrical
(shaped like half an egg)

Convex
(outwardly rounded)

Flat
(with top of uniform height)

Infundibuliform
(deeply, depressed, funnel-shaped)

Depressed
(with a low central region)

Umbonate
(with a central bump or knob)

Surface Markings (warts, scales, slime, etc.): _____

Cap Margin: Smooth, Inrolled, Sinuous/Wavy, Other: _____

Color Changes: _____

Undercap

Gills ○

Attachment: Free or Decurrent

Spacing: Crowded, Close, Distant, Subdistant

Color/Bruising: _____

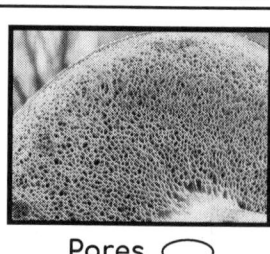

Pores ○

Color: _____

Pore Size: _____

Pore Pattern: _____

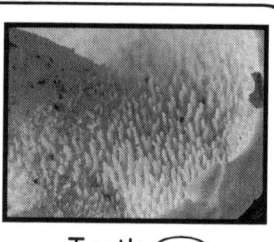

Teeth ○

Color: _____

Teeth Length: _____

Flesh: Soft or Tough

◯ Free
(gills not attached to stem)

◯ Adnexed
(gills attached narrowly to stem)

◯ Sinuate
(gills smoothly notched and running briefly down stem)

◯ Adnate
(gills widely attached widely to stem)

◯ Descending
(gills running down stem for some length)

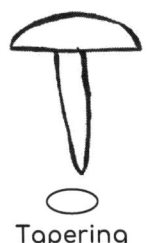  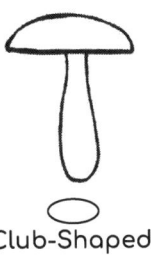 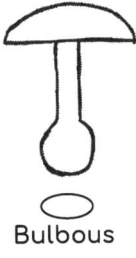 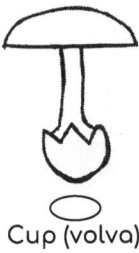

◯ Tapering

◯ Equal

◯ Club-Shaped

◯ Bulbous

◯ Cup (volva)

Morels
- Edible ☺
- Honeycombed cap
- Most morels cap is longer than stem
- Spore print is usually light colored
- Interior is hollow

Puffballs
- Edible ☺
- Color is white
- Rounded-shaped balls with or without spiny warts on top
- Can be mistaken for golf ball, baseball or even soccer ball

Fly Agaric
- Poisonous ☹
- Red-brown cap - irregularly lobed, like a brain
- Tube-like hollows
- Yellowish spore print
- Smooth with more wrinkles as it ages

Oyster Mushroom
- Edible ☺
- Grows on hardwood trees
- Gills descend to base
- Gills are not saw toothed or ruffled
- Spore deposit gray

Death Cap
- Poisonous ☹
- Flattened top
- White cap with brownish scales
- Gills are free and white, turning green as they mature

Jack O'Lantern
- Poisonous ☹
- Bright orange to yellowish
- Grows in clusters
- Cap convex
- Gills narrow
- Cream spore print

Lion's Mane
- Edible ☺
- Covered all over with long, spine-like hairs
- Club-shaped fruit bodies
- Common on hardwoods

Destroying Angel
- Poisonous ☹
- White stalk and gills
- White cap or white edge and yellowish, pinkish, or tan center
- Egg-shaped cap

Chicken of the Woods
- Edible ☺
- Fan-shaped and suede-like texture
- Fruitbody with yellow, round pores
- Brownish color

Chanterelle
- Edible ☺
- Shape looks like bell of a trumpet
- Bright yellow/orange
- Similar look to Jack o'Lantern

Deadly Galerina
- Poisonous ☹
- Brownish, sticky cap, yellowish to rusty gills, ring on stalk
- Edges are curved against gills
- Gills narrow, crowded

Witches' Butter
- Edible ☺
- Small, yellow, irregularly lobed, gelatinous masses
- Grows on dead deciduous wood, especially oaks

Spore Print

Location

Site / GPS: _____ Date: _____

◯ Living Tree ◯ Leaf Litter ◯ Mulch ◯ Dead Tree or Wood ◯ Grass
◯ Soil ◯ Other _____

Type of Tree(s) On or Near: _____

Forest Type: ◯ Deciduous ◯ Coniferous ◯ Tropical ◯ Other _____

Weather Conditions: _____

General

Size (overall height): _____ Color: _____ Spore Color: _____

Texture: ◯ Tough ◯ Brittle ◯ Leathery ◯ Woody ◯ Soft ◯ Slimy
◯ Spongy ◯ Powdery ◯ Waxy ◯ Rubbery ◯ Watery (Other) _____

Bruising When Touched? ◯ Yes ◯ No Notes: _____

Structures: ◯ Cup ◯ Ring ◯ Warts _____

Cap Characteristics

Campanulate
(bell-shaped)

Conical
(triangular)

Cylindrical
(shaped like half an egg)

Convex
(outwardly rounded)

Flat
(with top of
uniform height)

Infundibuliform
(deeply, depressed,
funnel-shaped)

Depressed
(with a low
central region)

Umbonate
(with a central
bump or knob)

Surface Markings (warts, scales, slime, etc.): _____

Cap Margin: Smooth, Inrolled, Sinuous/Wavy, Other: _____

Color Changes: _____

Undercap

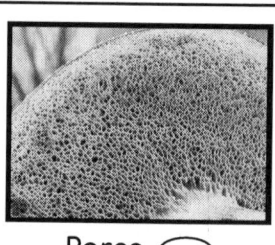

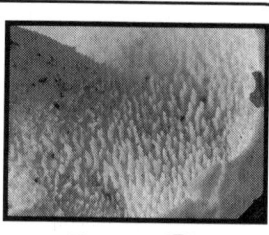

Gills ◯

Attachment: Free or Decurrent

Spacing: Crowded, Close,
Distant, Subdistant

Color/Bruising: _____

Pores ◯

Color: _____

Pore Size: _____

Pore Pattern: _____

Teeth ◯

Color: _____

Teeth Length: _____

Flesh: Soft or Tough

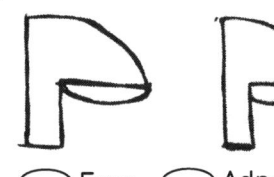

○ Free
(gills not attached to stem)

○ Adnexed
(gills attached narrowly to stem)

○ Sinuate
(gills smoothly notched and running briefly down stem)

○ Adnate
(gills widely attached widely to stem)

○ Descending
(gills running down stem for some length)

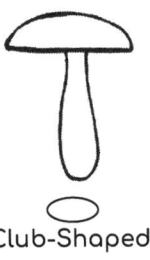
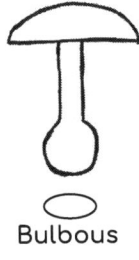
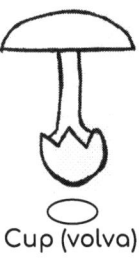

○ Tapering

○ Equal

○ Club-Shaped

○ Bulbous

○ Cup (volva)

Morels
- Edible ☺
- Honeycombed cap
- Most morels cap is longer than stem
- Spore print is usually light colored
- Interior is hollow

Puffballs
- Edible ☺
- Color is white
- Rounded-shaped balls with or without spiny warts on top
- Can be mistaken for golf ball, baseball or even soccer ball

Fly Agaric
- Poisonous ☹
- Red-brown cap - irregularly lobed, like a brain
- Tube-like hollows
- Yellowish spore print
- Smooth with more wrinkles as it ages

Oyster Mushroom
- Edible ☺
- Grows on hardwood trees
- Gills descend to base
- Gills are not saw toothed or ruffled
- Spore deposit gray

Death Cap
- Poisonous ☹
- Flattened top
- White cap with brownish scales
- Gills are free and white, turning green as they mature

Jack O'Lantern
- Poisonous ☹
- Bright orange to yellowish
- Grows in clusters
- Cap convex
- Gills narrow
- Cream spore print

Lion's Mane
- Edible ☺
- Covered all over with long, spine-like hairs
- Club-shaped fruit bodies
- Common on hardwoods

Destroying Angel
- Poisonous ☹
- White stalk and gills
- White cap or white edge and yellowish, pinkish, or tan center
- Egg-shaped cap

Chicken of the Woods
- Edible ☺
- Fan-shaped and suede-like texture
- Fruitbody with yellow, round pores
- Brownish color

Chanterelle
- Edible ☺
- Shape looks like bell of a trumpet
- Bright yellow/orange
- Similar look to Jack o'Lantern

Deadly Galerina
- Poisonous ☹
- Brownish, sticky cap, yellowish to rusty gills, ring on stalk
- Edges are curved against gills
- Gills narrow, crowded

Witches' Butter
- Edible ☺
- Small, yellow, irregularly lobed, gelatinous masses
- Grows on dead deciduous wood, especially oaks

Spore Print

_____

_____

_____

_____

_____

_____

Location

Site / GPS: _____ Date: _____

◯ Living Tree ◯ Leaf Litter ◯ Mulch ◯ Dead Tree or Wood ◯ Grass
◯ Soil ◯ Other _____

Type of Tree(s) On or Near: _____

Forest Type: ◯ Deciduous ◯ Coniferous ◯ Tropical ◯ Other _____

Weather Conditions: _____

General

Size (overall height): _____ Color: _____ Spore Color: _____

Texture: ◯ Tough ◯ Brittle ◯ Leathery ◯ Woody ◯ Soft ◯ Slimy
◯ Spongy ◯ Powdery ◯ Waxy ◯ Rubbery ◯ Watery (Other) _____

Bruising When Touched? ◯ Yes ◯ No Notes: _____

Structures: ◯ Cup ◯ Ring ◯ Warts _____

Cap Characteristics

Campanulate
(bell-shaped)

Conical
(triangular)

Cylindrical
(shaped like half an egg)

Convex
(outwardly rounded)

Flat
(with top of
uniform height)

Infundibuliform
(deeply, depressed,
funnel-shaped)

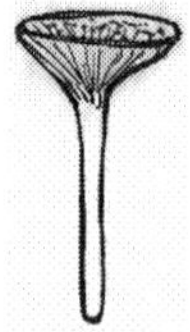

Depressed
(with a low
central region)

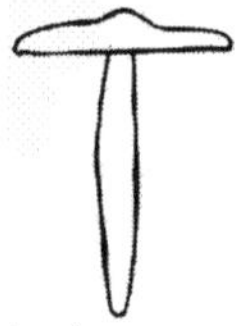

Umbonate
(with a central
bump or knob)

Surface Markings (warts, scales, slime, etc.): _____

Cap Margin: Smooth, Inrolled, Sinuous/Wavy, Other: _____

Color Changes: _____

Undercap

Gills ◯

Attachment: Free or Decurrent

Spacing: Crowded, Close,
Distant, Subdistant

Color/Bruising: _____

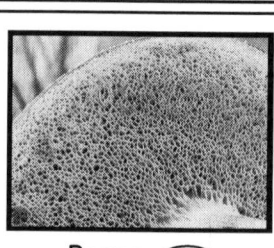

Pores ◯

Color: _____

Pore Size: _____

Pore Pattern: _____

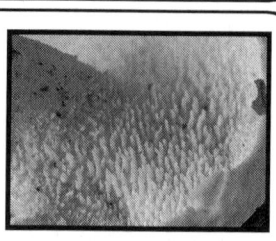

Teeth ◯

Color: _____

Teeth Length: _____

Flesh: Soft or Tough

○ Free
(gills not attached to stem)

○ Adnexed
(gills attached narrowly to stem)

○ Sinuate
(gills smoothly notched and running briefly down stem)

○ Adnate
(gills widely attached widely to stem)

○ Descending
(gills running down stem for some length)

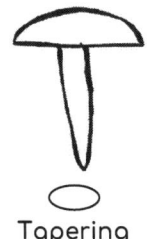  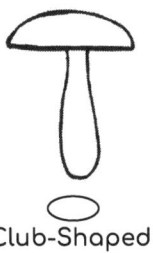 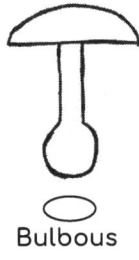 

Tapering   Equal   Club-Shaped   Bulbous   Cup (volva)

Morels
- Edible ☺
- Honeycombed cap
- Most morels cap is longer than stem
- Spore print is usually light colored
- Interior is hollow

Puffballs
- Edible ☺
- Color is white
- Rounded-shaped balls with or without spiny warts on top
- Can be mistaken for golf ball, baseball or even soccer ball

Fly Agaric
- Poisonous ☹
- Red-brown cap - irregularly lobed, like a brain
- Tube-like hollows
- Yellowish spore print
- Smooth with more wrinkles as it ages

Oyster Mushroom
- Edible ☺
- Grows on hardwood trees
- Gills descend to base
- Gills are not saw toothed or ruffled
- Spore deposit gray

Death Cap
- Poisonous ☹
- Flattened top
- White cap with brownish scales
- Gills are free and white, turning green as they mature

Jack O'Lantern
- Poisonous ☹
- Bright orange to yellowish
- Grows in clusters
- Cap convex
- Gills narrow
- Cream spore print

Lion's Mane
- Edible ☺
- Covered all over with long, spine-like hairs
- Club-shaped fruit bodies
- Common on hardwoods

Destroying Angel
- Poisonous ☹
- White stalk and gills
- White cap or white edge and yellowish, pinkish, or tan center
- Egg-shaped cap

Chicken of the Woods
- Edible ☺
- Fan-shaped and suede-like texture
- Fruitbody with yellow, round pores
- Brownish color

Chanterelle
- Edible ☺
- Shape looks like bell of a trumpet
- Bright yellow/orange
- Similar look to Jack o'Lantern

Deadly Galerina
- Poisonous ☹
- Brownish, sticky cap, yellowish to rusty gills, ring on stalk
- Edges are curved against gills
- Gills narrow, crowded

Witches' Butter
- Edible ☺
- Small, yellow, irregularly lobed, gelatinous masses
- Grows on dead deciduous wood, especially oaks

Spore Print

_____

_____

_____

_____

_____

_____

Location

Site / GPS: _____ Date: _____

○ Living Tree ○ Leaf Litter ○ Mulch ○ Dead Tree or Wood ○ Grass
○ Soil ○ Other _____

Type of Tree(s) On or Near: _____

Forest Type: ○ Deciduous ○ Coniferous ○ Tropical ○ Other _____

Weather Conditions: _____

General

Size (overall height): _____ Color: _____ Spore Color: _____

Texture: ○ Tough ○ Brittle ○ Leathery ○ Woody ○ Soft ○ Slimy
○ Spongy ○ Powdery ○ Waxy ○ Rubbery ○ Watery (Other) _____

Bruising When Touched? ○ Yes ○ No   Notes: _____

Structures: ○ Cup ○ Ring ○ Warts   _____

Cap Characteristics

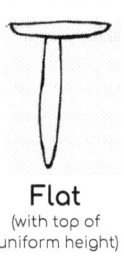

Campanulate
(bell-shaped)

Conical
(triangular)

Cylindrical
(shaped like half an egg)

Convex
(outwardly rounded)

   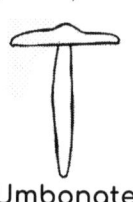

Flat
(with top of
uniform height)

Infundibuliform
(deeply, depressed,
funnel-shaped)

Depressed
(with a low
central region)

Umbonate
(with a central
bump or knob)

Surface Markings (warts, scales, slime, etc.): _____

Cap Margin: Smooth, Inrolled, Sinuous/Wavy, Other:_____

Color Changes: _____

Undercap

 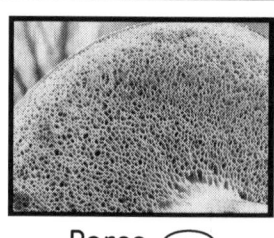 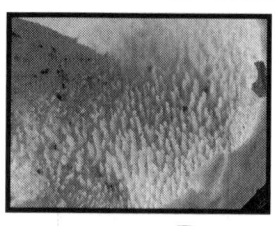

Gills ○

Attachment: Free or Decurrent

Spacing: Crowded, Close,
Distant, Subdistant

Color/Bruising: _____

Pores ○

Color: _____

Pore Size: _____

Pore Pattern: _____

Teeth ○

Color: _____

Teeth Length: _____

Flesh: Soft or Tough

Free	Adnexed	Sinuate	Adnate	Descending
(gills not attached to stem)	(gills attached narrowly to stem)	(gills smoothly notched and running briefly down stem)	(gills widely attached widely to stem)	(gills running down stem for some length)

  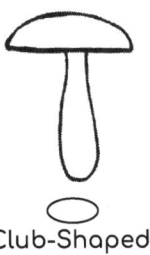 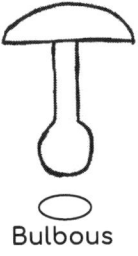 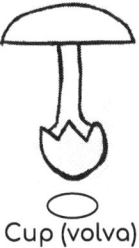

| Tapering | Equal | Club-Shaped | Bulbous | Cup (volva) |

Morels
- Edible ☺
- Honeycombed cap
- Most morels cap is longer than stem
- Spore print is usually light colored
- Interior is hollow

Puffballs
- Edible ☺
- Color is white
- Rounded-shaped balls with or without spiny warts on top
- Can be mistaken for golf ball, baseball or even soccer ball

Fly Agaric
- Poisonous ☹
- Red-brown cap - irregularly lobed, like a brain
- Tube-like hollows
- Yellowish spore print
- Smooth with more wrinkles as it ages

Oyster Mushroom
- Edible ☺
- Grows on hardwood trees
- Gills descend to base
- Gills are not saw toothed or ruffled
- Spore deposit gray

Death Cap
- Poisonous ☹
- Flattened top
- White cap with brownish scales
- Gills are free and white, turning green as they mature

Jack O'Lantern
- Poisonous ☹
- Bright orange to yellowish
- Grows in clusters
- Cap convex
- Gills narrow
- Cream spore print

Lion's Mane
- Edible ☺
- Covered all over with long, spine-like hairs
- Club-shaped fruit bodies
- Common on hardwoods

Destroying Angel
- Poisonous ☹
- White stalk and gills
- White cap or white edge and yellowish, pinkish, or tan center
- Egg-shaped cap

Chicken of the Woods
- Edible ☺
- Fan-shaped and suede-like texture
- Fruitbody with yellow, round pores
- Brownish color

Chanterelle
- Edible ☺
- Shape looks like bell of a trumpet
- Bright yellow/orange
- Similar look to Jack o'Lantern

Deadly Galerina
- Poisonous ☹
- Brownish, sticky cap, yellowish to rusty gills, ring on stalk
- Edges are curved against gills
- Gills narrow, crowded

Witches' Butter
- Edible ☺
- Small, yellow, irregularly lobed, gelatinous masses
- Grows on dead deciduous wood, especially oaks

Spore Print

_____

_____

_____

_____

_____

_____

Location

Site / GPS: _____ Date: _____

○ Living Tree   ○ Leaf Litter   ○ Mulch   ○ Dead Tree or Wood   ○ Grass
○ Soil   ○ Other _____

Type of Tree(s) On or Near: _____

Forest Type: ○ Deciduous   ○ Coniferous   ○ Tropical   ○ Other _____

Weather Conditions: _____

General

Size (overall height): _____ Color: _____ Spore Color: _____

Texture: ○ Tough ○ Brittle ○ Leathery ○ Woody ○ Soft ○ Slimy
○ Spongy ○ Powdery ○ Waxy ○ Rubbery ○ Watery (Other) _____

Bruising When Touched? ○ Yes ○ No   Notes: _____

Structures: ○ Cup ○ Ring ○ Warts   _____

Cap Characteristics

Campanulate
(bell-shaped)

Conical
(triangular)

Cylindrical
(shaped like half an egg)

Convex
(outwardly rounded)

Flat
(with top of uniform height)

Infundibuliform
(deeply, depressed, funnel-shaped)

Depressed
(with a low central region)

Umbonate
(with a central bump or knob)

Surface Markings (warts, scales, slime, etc.): _____

Cap Margin: Smooth, Inrolled, Sinuous/Wavy, Other: _____

Color Changes: _____

Undercap

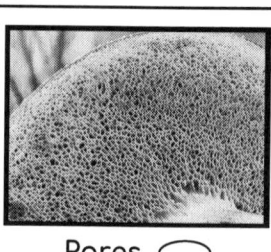

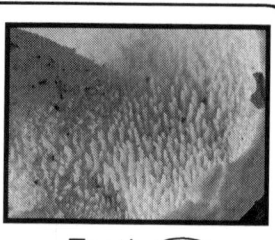

Gills ○
Attachment: Free or Decurrent
Spacing: Crowded, Close, Distant, Subdistant
Color/Bruising: _____

Pores ○
Color: _____
Pore Size: _____
Pore Pattern: _____

Teeth ○
Color: _____
Teeth Length: _____
Flesh: Soft or Tough

Free
(gills not attached to stem)

Adnexed
(gills attached narrowly to stem)

Sinuate
(gills smoothly notched and running briefly down stem)

Adnate
(gills widely attached widely to stem)

Descenting
(gills running down stem for some length)

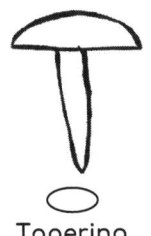

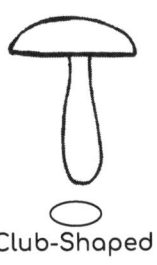
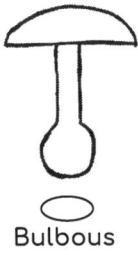

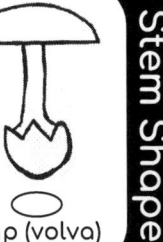

Tapering   **Equal**   **Club-Shaped**   **Bulbous**   **Cup (volva)**

Morels

- Edible ☺
- Honeycombed cap
- Most morels cap is longer than stem
- Spore print is usually light colored
- Interior is hollow

Puffballs

- Edible ☺
- Color is white
- Rounded-shaped balls with or without spiny warts on top
- Can be mistaken for golf ball, baseball or even soccer ball

Fly Agaric

- Poisonous ☹
- Red-brown cap - irregularly lobed, like a brain
- Tube-like hollows
- Yellowish spore print
- Smooth with more wrinkles as it ages

Oyster Mushroom

- Edible ☺
- Grows on hardwood trees
- Gills descend to base
- Gills are not saw toothed or ruffled
- Spore deposit gray

Death Cap

- Poisonous ☹
- Flattened top
- White cap with brownish scales
- Gills are free and white, turning green as they mature

Jack O'Lantern

- Poisonous ☹
- Bright orange to yellowish
- Grows in clusters
- Cap convex
- Gills narrow
- Cream spore print

Lion's Mane

- Edible ☺
- Covered all over with long, spine-like hairs
- Club-shaped fruit bodies
- Common on hardwoods

Destroying Angel

- Poisonous ☹
- White stalk and gills
- White cap or white edge and yellowish, pinkish, or tan center
- Egg-shaped cap

Chicken of the Woods

- Edible ☺
- Fan-shaped and suede-like texture
- Fruitbody with yellow, round pores
- Brownish color

Chanterelle

- Edible ☺
- Shape looks like bell of a trumpet
- Bright yellow/orange
- Similar look to Jack o'Lantern

Deadly Galerina

- Poisonous ☹
- Brownish, sticky cap, yellowish to rusty gills, ring on stalk
- Edges are curved against gills
- Gills narrow, crowded

Witches' Butter

- Edible ☺
- Small, yellow, irregularly lobed, gelatinous masses
- Grows on dead deciduous wood, especially oaks

Spore Print

_____
_____
_____
_____
_____
_____

Location

Site / GPS: _____ Date: _____

○ Living Tree　○ Leaf Litter　○ Mulch　○ Dead Tree or Wood　○ Grass
○ Soil　○ Other _____

Type of Tree(s) On or Near: _____

Forest Type: ○ Deciduous　○ Coniferous　○ Tropical　○ Other _____

Weather Conditions: _____

General

Size (overall height): _____ Color: _____ Spore Color: _____

Texture: ○ Tough　○ Brittle　○ Leathery　○ Woody　○ Soft　○ Slimy
○ Spongy　○ Powdery　○ Waxy　○ Rubbery　○ Watery　(Other) _____

Bruising When Touched? ○ Yes　○ No　Notes: _____

Structures: ○ Cup　○ Ring　○ Warts　　　_____

Cap Characteristics

Campanulate
(bell-shaped)

Conical
(triangular)

Cylindrical
(shaped like half an egg)

Convex
(outwardly rounded)

Flat
(with top of
uniform height)

Infundibuliform
(deeply, depressed,
funnel-shaped)

Depressed
(with a low
central region)

Umbonate
(with a central
bump or knob)

Surface Markings (warts, scales, slime, etc.): _____

Cap Margin: Smooth, Inrolled, Sinuous/Wavy, Other:_____

Color Changes: _____

Undercap

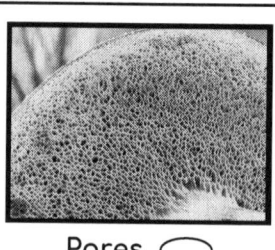

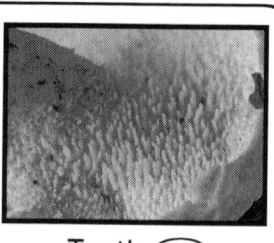

Gills ○

Attachment: Free or Decurrent

Spacing: Crowded, Close,
Distant, Subdistant

Color/Bruising: _____

Pores ○

Color: _____

Pore Size: _____

Pore Pattern:_____

Teeth ○

Color: _____

Teeth Length: _____

Flesh: Soft or Tough

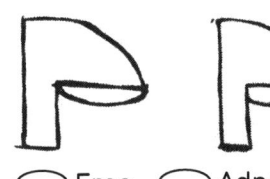

○ Free
(gills not attached to stem)

○ Adnexed
(gills attached narrowly to stem)

○ Sinuate
(gills smoothly notched and running briefly down stem)

○ Adnate
(gills widely attached widely to stem)

○ Descending
(gills running down stem for some length)

Tapering

Equal

Club-Shaped

Bulbous

Cup (volva)

Morels
- Edible ☺
- Honeycombed cap
- Most morels cap is longer than stem
- Spore print is usually light colored
- Interior is hollow

Puffballs
- Edible ☺
- Color is white
- Rounded-shaped balls with or without spiny warts on top
- Can be mistaken for golf ball, baseball or even soccer ball

Fly Agaric
- Poisonous ☹
- Red-brown cap - irregularly lobed, like a brain
- Tube-like hollows
- Yellowish spore print
- Smooth with more wrinkles as it ages

Oyster Mushroom
- Edible ☺
- Grows on hardwood trees
- Gills descend to base
- Gills are not saw toothed or ruffled
- Spore deposit gray

Death Cap
- Poisonous ☹
- Flattened top
- White cap with brownish scales
- Gills are free and white, turning green as they mature

Jack O'Lantern
- Poisonous ☹
- Bright orange to yellowish
- Grows in clusters
- Cap convex
- Gills narrow
- Cream spore print

Lion's Mane
- Edible ☺
- Covered all over with long, spine-like hairs
- Club-shaped fruit bodies
- Common on hardwoods

Destroying Angel
- Poisonous ☹
- White stalk and gills
- White cap or white edge and yellowish, pinkish, or tan center
- Egg-shaped cap

Chicken of the Woods
- Edible ☺
- Fan-shaped and suede-like texture
- Fruitbody with yellow, round pores
- Brownish color

Chanterelle
- Edible ☺
- Shape looks like bell of a trumpet
- Bright yellow/orange
- Similar look to Jack o'Lantern

Deadly Galerina
- Poisonous ☹
- Brownish, sticky cap, yellowish to rusty gills, ring on stalk
- Edges are curved against gills
- Gills narrow, crowded

Witches' Butter
- Edible ☺
- Small, yellow, irregularly lobed, gelatinous masses
- Grows on dead deciduous wood, especially oaks

Spore Print

_____

_____

_____

_____

_____

_____

Location

Site / GPS: _____ Date: _____

○ Living Tree ○ Leaf Litter ○ Mulch ○ Dead Tree or Wood ○ Grass
○ Soil ○ Other _____

Type of Tree(s) On or Near: _____

Forest Type: ○ Deciduous ○ Coniferous ○ Tropical ○ Other _____

Weather Conditions: _____

General

Size (overall height): _____ Color: _____ Spore Color: _____

Texture: ○ Tough ○ Brittle ○ Leathery ○ Woody ○ Soft ○ Slimy
○ Spongy ○ Powdery ○ Waxy ○ Rubbery ○ Watery (Other) _____

Bruising When Touched? ○ Yes ○ No   Notes: _____

Structures: ○ Cup ○ Ring ○ Warts   _____

Cap Characteristics

Campanulate
(bell-shaped)

Conical
(triangular)

Cylindrical
(shaped like half an egg)

Convex
(outwardly rounded)

Flat
(with top of
uniform height)

Infundibuliform
(deeply, depressed,
funnel-shaped)

Depressed
(with a low
central region)

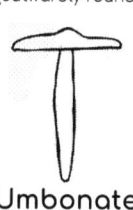

Umbonate
(with a central
bump or knob)

Surface Markings (warts, scales, slime, etc.): _____

Cap Margin: Smooth, Inrolled, Sinuous/Wavy, Other: _____

Color Changes: _____

Undercap

Gills ○

Attachment: Free or Decurrent

Spacing: Crowded, Close,
          Distant, Subdistant

Color/Bruising: _____

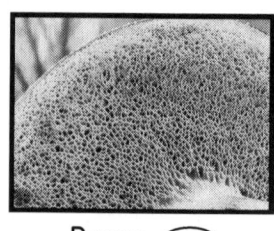

Pores ○

Color: _____

Pore Size: _____

Pore Pattern: _____

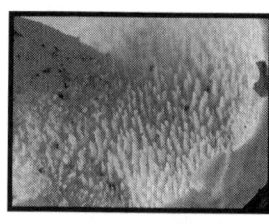

Teeth ○

Color: _____

Teeth Length: _____

Flesh: Soft or Tough

⬭ Free
(gills not attached to stem)

⬭ Adnexed
(gills attached narrowly to stem)

⬭ Sinuate
(gills smoothly notched and running briefly down stem)

⬭ Adnate
(gills widely attached widely to stem)

⬭ Descenting
(gills running down stem for some length)

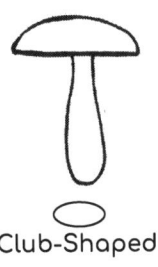
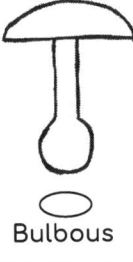

⬭ Tapering

⬭ Equal

⬭ Club-Shaped

⬭ Bulbous

⬭ Cup (volva)

Morels
- Edible ☺
- Honeycombed cap
- Most morels cap is longer than stem
- Spore print is usually light colored
- Interior is hollow

Puffballs
- Edible ☺
- Color is white
- Rounded-shaped balls with or without spiny warts on top
- Can be mistaken for golf ball, baseball or even soccer ball

Fly Agaric
- Poisonous ☹
- Red-brown cap - irregularly lobed, like a brain
- Tube-like hollows
- Yellowish spore print
- Smooth with more wrinkles as it ages

Oyster Mushroom
- Edible ☺
- Grows on hardwood trees
- Gills descend to base
- Gills are not saw toothed or ruffled
- Spore deposit gray

Death Cap
- Poisonous ☹
- Flattened top
- White cap with brownish scales
- Gills are free and white, turning green as they mature

Jack O'Lantern
- Poisonous ☹
- Bright orange to yellowish
- Grows in clusters
- Cap convex
- Gills narrow
- Cream spore print

Lion's Mane
- Edible ☺
- Covered all over with long, spine-like hairs
- Club-shaped fruit bodies
- Common on hardwoods

Destroying Angel
- Poisonous ☹
- White stalk and gills
- White cap or white edge and yellowish, pinkish, or tan center
- Egg-shaped cap

Chicken of the Woods
- Edible ☺
- Fan-shaped and suede-like texture
- Fruitbody with yellow, round pores
- Brownish color

Chanterelle
- Edible ☺
- Shape looks like bell of a trumpet
- Bright yellow/orange
- Similar look to Jack o'Lantern

Deadly Galerina
- Poisonous ☹
- Brownish, sticky cap, yellowish to rusty gills, ring on stalk
- Edges are curved against gills
- Gills narrow, crowded

Witches' Butter
- Edible ☺
- Small, yellow, irregularly lobed, gelatinous masses
- Grows on dead deciduous wood, especially oaks

Spore Print

_____

_____

_____

_____

_____

_____

Location

Site / GPS: _____ Date: _____

◯ Living Tree   ◯ Leaf Litter   ◯ Mulch   ◯ Dead Tree or Wood   ◯ Grass
◯ Soil   ◯ Other _____

Type of Tree(s) On or Near: _____

Forest Type: ◯ Deciduous   ◯ Coniferous   ◯ Tropical   ◯ Other _____

Weather Conditions: _____

General

Size (overall height): _____   Color: _____   Spore Color: _____

Texture: ◯ Tough   ◯ Brittle   ◯ Leathery   ◯ Woody   ◯ Soft   ◯ Slimy
◯ Spongy   ◯ Powdery   ◯ Waxy   ◯ Rubbery   ◯ Watery   (Other) _____

Bruising When Touched? ◯ Yes   ◯ No   Notes: _____

Structures: ◯ Cup   ◯ Ring   ◯ Warts   _____

Cap Characteristics

Campanulate
(bell-shaped)

Conical
(triangular)

Cylindrical
(shaped like half an egg)

Convex
(outwardly rounded)

Flat
(with top of
uniform height)

Infundibuliform
(deeply, depressed,
funnel-shaped)

Depressed
(with a low
central region)

Umbonate
(with a central
bump or knob)

Surface Markings (warts, scales, slime, etc.): _____

Cap Margin: Smooth, Inrolled, Sinuous/Wavy, Other: _____

Color Changes: _____

Undercap

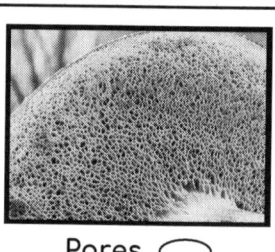

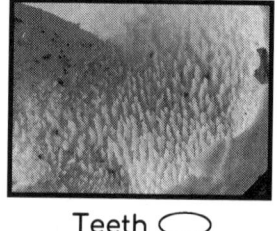

Gills ◯

Attachment: Free or Decurrent

Spacing: Crowded, Close,
Distant, Subdistant

Color/Bruising: _____

Pores ◯

Color: _____

Pore Size: _____

Pore Pattern: _____

Teeth ◯

Color: _____

Teeth Length: _____

Flesh: Soft or Tough

○ Free
(gills not attached to stem)

○ Adnexed
(gills attached narrowly to stem)

○ Sinuate
(gills smoothly notched and running briefly down stem)

○ Adnate
(gills widely attached widely to stem)

○ Descending
(gills running down stem for some length)

Tapering   Equal   Club-Shaped   Bulbous   Cup (volva)

Morels
- Edible ☺
- Honeycombed cap
- Most morels cap is longer than stem
- Spore print is usually light colored
- Interior is hollow

Puffballs
- Edible ☺
- Color is white
- Rounded-shaped balls with or without spiny warts on top
- Can be mistaken for golf ball, baseball or even soccer ball

Fly Agaric
- Poisonous ☹
- Red-brown cap - irregularly lobed, like a brain
- Tube-like hollows
- Yellowish spore print
- Smooth with more wrinkles as it ages

Oyster Mushroom
- Edible ☺
- Grows on hardwood trees
- Gills descend to base
- Gills are not saw toothed or ruffled
- Spore deposit gray

Death Cap
- Poisonous ☹
- Flattened top
- White cap with brownish scales
- Gills are free and white, turning green as they mature

Jack O'Lantern
- Poisonous ☹
- Bright orange to yellowish
- Grows in clusters
- Cap convex
- Gills narrow
- Cream spore print

Lion's Mane
- Edible ☺
- Covered all over with long, spine-like hairs
- Club-shaped fruit bodies
- Common on hardwoods

Destroying Angel
- Poisonous ☹
- White stalk and gills
- White cap or white edge and yellowish, pinkish, or tan center
- Egg-shaped cap

Chicken of the Woods
- Edible ☺
- Fan-shaped and suede-like texture
- Fruitbody with yellow, round pores
- Brownish color

Chanterelle
- Edible ☺
- Shape looks like bell of a trumpet
- Bright yellow/orange
- Similar look to Jack o'Lantern

Deadly Galerina
- Poisonous ☹
- Brownish, sticky cap, yellowish to rusty gills, ring on stalk
- Edges are curved against gills
- Gills narrow, crowded

Witches' Butter
- Edible ☺
- Small, yellow, irregularly lobed, gelatinous masses
- Grows on dead deciduous wood, especially oaks

Spore Print

_____
_____
_____
_____
_____
_____

Location

Site / GPS: _____ Date: _____

○ Living Tree ○ Leaf Litter ○ Mulch ○ Dead Tree or Wood ○ Grass
○ Soil ○ Other _____

Type of Tree(s) On or Near: _____

Forest Type: ○ Deciduous ○ Coniferous ○ Tropical ○ Other _____

Weather Conditions: _____

General

Size (overall height): _____ Color: _____ Spore Color: _____

Texture: ○ Tough ○ Brittle ○ Leathery ○ Woody ○ Soft ○ Slimy
○ Spongy ○ Powdery ○ Waxy ○ Rubbery ○ Watery (Other) _____

Bruising When Touched? ○ Yes ○ No   Notes: _____

Structures: ○ Cup ○ Ring ○ Warts   _____

Cap Characteristics

Campanulate
(bell-shaped)

Conical
(triangular)

Cylindrical
(shaped like half an egg)

Convex
(outwardly rounded)

Flat
(with top of uniform height)

Infundibuliform
(deeply, depressed, funnel-shaped)

Depressed
(with a low central region)

Umbonate
(with a central bump or knob)

Surface Markings (warts, scales, slime, etc.): _____

Cap Margin: Smooth, Inrolled, Sinuous/Wavy, Other: _____

Color Changes: _____

Undercap

Gills ○

Attachment: Free or Decurrent

Spacing: Crowded, Close, Distant, Subdistant

Color/Bruising: _____

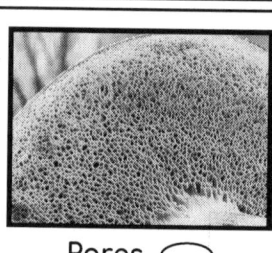

Pores ○

Color: _____

Pore Size: _____

Pore Pattern: _____

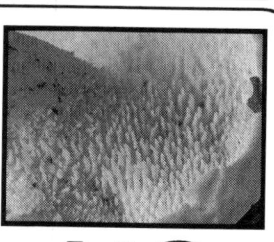

Teeth ○

Color: _____

Teeth Length: _____

Flesh: Soft or Tough

◯ Free
(gills not attached to stem)

◯ Adnexed
(gills attached narrowly to stem)

◯ Sinuate
(gills smoothly notched and running briefly down stem)

◯ Adnate
(gills widely attached widely to stem)

◯ Descending
(gills running down stem for some length)

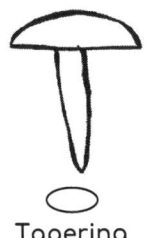  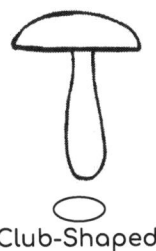 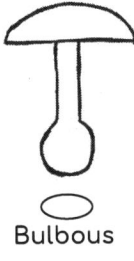 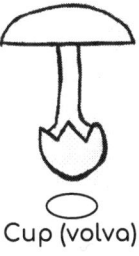

◯ Tapering

◯ Equal

◯ Club-Shaped

◯ Bulbous

◯ Cup (volva)

Morels
- Edible ☺
- Honeycombed cap
- Most morels cap is longer than stem
- Spore print is usually light colored
- Interior is hollow

Puffballs
- Edible ☺
- Color is white
- Rounded-shaped balls with or without spiny warts on top
- Can be mistaken for golf ball, baseball or even soccer ball

Fly Agaric
- Poisonous ☹
- Red-brown cap - irregularly lobed, like a brain
- Tube-like hollows
- Yellowish spore print
- Smooth with more wrinkles as it ages

Oyster Mushroom
- Edible ☺
- Grows on hardwood trees
- Gills descend to base
- Gills are not saw toothed or ruffled
- Spore deposit gray

Death Cap
- Poisonous ☹
- Flattened top
- White cap with brownish scales
- Gills are free and white, turning green as they mature

Jack O'Lantern
- Poisonous ☹
- Bright orange to yellowish
- Grows in clusters
- Cap convex
- Gills narrow
- Cream spore print

Lion's Mane
- Edible ☺
- Covered all over with long, spine-like hairs
- Club-shaped fruit bodies
- Common on hardwoods

Destroying Angel
- Poisonous ☹
- White stalk and gills
- White cap or white edge and yellowish, pinkish, or tan center
- Egg-shaped cap

Chicken of the Woods
- Edible ☺
- Fan-shaped and suede-like texture
- Fruitbody with yellow, round pores
- Brownish color

Chanterelle
- Edible ☺
- Shape looks like bell of a trumpet
- Bright yellow/orange
- Similar look to Jack o'Lantern

Deadly Galerina
- Poisonous ☹
- Brownish, sticky cap, yellowish to rusty gills, ring on stalk
- Edges are curved against gills
- Gills narrow, crowded

Witches' Butter
- Edible ☺
- Small, yellow, irregularly lobed, gelatinous masses
- Grows on dead deciduous wood, especially oaks

Spore Print

_____

_____

_____

_____

_____

_____

Location

Site / GPS: _____ Date: _____

◯ Living Tree   ◯ Leaf Litter   ◯ Mulch   ◯ Dead Tree or Wood   ◯ Grass

◯ Soil   ◯ Other _____

Type of Tree(s) On or Near: _____

Forest Type: ◯ Deciduous   ◯ Coniferous   ◯ Tropical   ◯ Other _____

Weather Conditions: _____

General

Size (overall height): _____   Color: _____   Spore Color: _____

Texture: ◯ Tough   ◯ Brittle   ◯ Leathery   ◯ Woody   ◯ Soft   ◯ Slimy

◯ Spongy   ◯ Powdery   ◯ Waxy   ◯ Rubbery   ◯ Watery   (Other) _____

Bruising When Touched? ◯ Yes   ◯ No   Notes: _____

Structures: ◯ Cup   ◯ Ring   ◯ Warts   _____

Cap Characteristics

Campanulate
(bell-shaped)

Conical
(triangular)

Cylindrical
(shaped like half an egg)

Convex
(outwardly rounded)

Flat
(with top of uniform height)

Infundibuliform
(deeply, depressed, funnel-shaped)

Depressed
(with a low central region)

Umbonate
(with a central bump or knob)

Surface Markings (warts, scales, slime, etc.): _____

Cap Margin: Smooth, Inrolled, Sinuous/Wavy, Other: _____

Color Changes: _____

Undercap

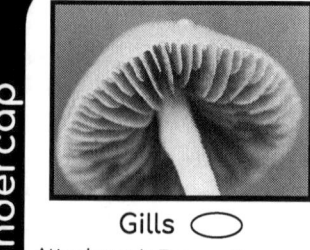

Gills ◯

Attachment: Free or Decurrent

Spacing: Crowded, Close, Distant, Subdistant

Color/Bruising: _____

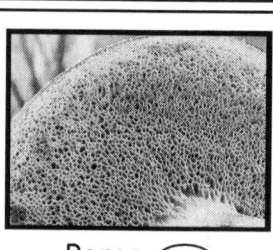

Pores ◯

Color: _____

Pore Size: _____

Pore Pattern: _____

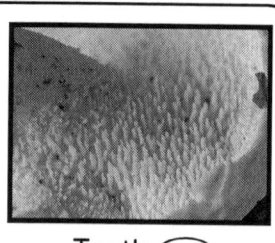

Teeth ◯

Color: _____

Teeth Length: _____

Flesh: Soft or Tough

○ **Free**
(gills not attached to stem)

○ **Adnexed**
(gills attached narrowly to stem)

○ **Sinuate**
(gills smoothly notched and running briefly down stem)

○ **Adnate**
(gills widely attached widely to stem)

○ **Descending**
(gills running down stem for some length)

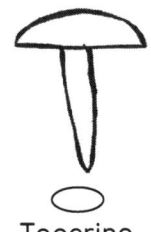  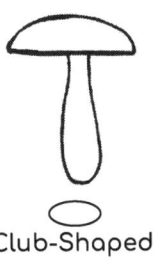 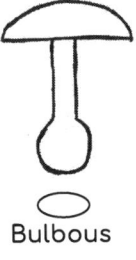 

○ **Tapering**   ○ **Equal**   ○ **Club-Shaped**   ○ **Bulbous**   ○ **Cup (volva)**

Morels
- Edible ☺
- Honeycombed cap
- Most morels cap is longer than stem
- Spore print is usually light colored
- Interior is hollow

Puffballs
- Edible ☺
- Color is white
- Rounded-shaped balls with or without spiny warts on top
- Can be mistaken for golf ball, baseball or even soccer ball

Fly Agaric
- Poisonous ☹
- Red-brown cap - irregularly lobed, like a brain
- Tube-like hollows
- Yellowish spore print
- Smooth with more wrinkles as it ages

Oyster Mushroom
- Edible ☺
- Grows on hardwood trees
- Gills descend to base
- Gills are not saw toothed or ruffled
- Spore deposit gray

Death Cap
- Poisonous ☹
- Flattened top
- White cap with brownish scales
- Gills are free and white, turning green as they mature

Jack O'Lantern
- Poisonous ☹
- Bright orange to yellowish
- Grows in clusters
- Cap convex
- Gills narrow
- Cream spore print

Lion's Mane
- Edible ☺
- Covered all over with long, spine-like hairs
- Club-shaped fruit bodies
- Common on hardwoods

Destroying Angel
- Poisonous ☹
- White stalk and gills
- White cap or white edge and yellowish, pinkish, or tan center
- Egg-shaped cap

Chicken of the Woods
- Edible ☺
- Fan-shaped and suede-like texture
- Fruitbody with yellow, round pores
- Brownish color

Chanterelle
- Edible ☺
- Shape looks like bell of a trumpet
- Bright yellow/orange
- Similar look to Jack o'Lantern

Deadly Galerina
- Poisonous ☹
- Brownish, sticky cap, yellowish to rusty gills, ring on stalk
- Edges are curved against gills
- Gills narrow, crowded

Witches' Butter
- Edible ☺
- Small, yellow, irregularly lobed, gelatinous masses
- Grows on dead deciduous wood, especially oaks

Spore Print

_____

_____

_____

_____

_____

_____

Location

Site / GPS: _____ Date: _____

○ Living Tree   ○ Leaf Litter   ○ Mulch   ○ Dead Tree or Wood   ○ Grass
○ Soil   ○ Other _____

Type of Tree(s) On or Near: _____

Forest Type: ○ Deciduous   ○ Coniferous   ○ Tropical   ○ Other _____

Weather Conditions: _____

General

Size (overall height): _____   Color: _____   Spore Color: _____

Texture: ○ Tough   ○ Brittle   ○ Leathery   ○ Woody   ○ Soft   ○ Slimy
○ Spongy   ○ Powdery   ○ Waxy   ○ Rubbery   ○ Watery   (Other) _____

Bruising When Touched?   ○ Yes   ○ No   Notes: _____

Structures: ○ Cup   ○ Ring   ○ Warts   _____

Cap Characteristics

Campanulate
(bell-shaped)

Conical
(triangular)

Cylindrical
(shaped like half an egg)

Convex
(outwardly rounded)

Flat
(with top of
uniform height)

Infundibuliform
(deeply, depressed,
funnel-shaped)

Depressed
(with a low
central region)

Umbonate
(with a central
bump or knob)

Surface Markings (warts, scales, slime, etc.): _____

Cap Margin: Smooth, Inrolled, Sinuous/Wavy, Other: _____

Color Changes: _____

Undercap

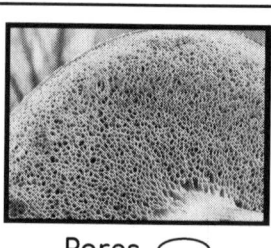

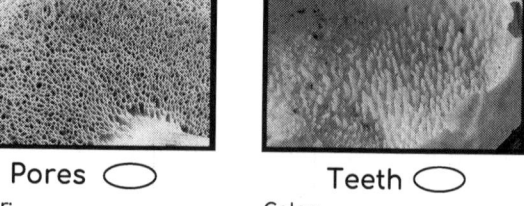

Gills ○

Attachment: Free or Decurrent

Spacing: Crowded, Close,
Distant, Subdistant

Color/Bruising: _____

Pores ○

Color: _____

Pore Size: _____

Pore Pattern: _____

Teeth ○

Color: _____

Teeth Length: _____

Flesh: Soft or Tough

◯ Free	◯ Adnexed	◯ Sinuate	◯ Adnate	◯ Descending
(gills not attached to stem)	(gills attached narrowly to stem)	(gills smoothly notched and running briefly down stem)	(gills widely attached widely to stem)	(gills running down stem for some length)

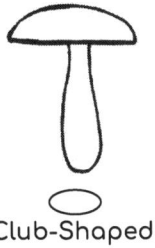
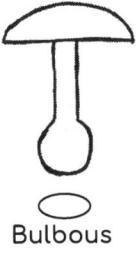
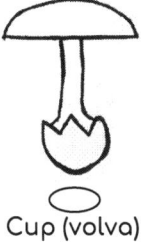

◯ Tapering	◯ Equal	◯ Club-Shaped	◯ Bulbous	◯ Cup (volva)

Morels

- Edible ☺
- Honeycombed cap
- Most morels cap is longer than stem
- Spore print is usually light colored
- Interior is hollow

Puffballs

- Edible ☺
- Color is white
- Rounded-shaped balls with or without spiny warts on top
- Can be mistaken for golf ball, baseball or even soccer ball

Fly Agaric

- Poisonous ☹
- Red-brown cap - irregularly lobed, like a brain
- Tube-like hollows
- Yellowish spore print
- Smooth with more wrinkles as it ages

Oyster Mushroom

- Edible ☺
- Grows on hardwood trees
- Gills descend to base
- Gills are not saw toothed or ruffled
- Spore deposit gray

Death Cap

- Poisonous ☹
- Flattened top
- White cap with brownish scales
- Gills are free and white, turning green as they mature

Jack O'Lantern

- Poisonous ☹
- Bright orange to yellowish
- Grows in clusters
- Cap convex
- Gills narrow
- Cream spore print

Lion's Mane

- Edible ☺
- Covered all over with long, spine-like hairs
- Club-shaped fruit bodies
- Common on hardwoods

Destroying Angel

- Poisonous ☹
- White stalk and gills
- White cap or white edge and yellowish, pinkish, or tan center
- Egg-shaped cap

Chicken of the Woods

- Edible ☺
- Fan-shaped and suede-like texture
- Fruitbody with yellow, round pores
- Brownish color

Chanterelle

- Edible ☺
- Shape looks like bell of a trumpet
- Bright yellow/orange
- Similar look to Jack o'Lantern

Deadly Galerina

- Poisonous ☹
- Brownish, sticky cap, yellowish to rusty gills, ring on stalk
- Edges are curved against gills
- Gills narrow, crowded

Witches' Butter

- Edible ☺
- Small, yellow, irregularly lobed, gelatinous masses
- Grows on dead deciduous wood, especially oaks

Spore Print

_____

_____

_____

_____

_____

Location

Site / GPS: _____ Date: _____

○ Living Tree ○ Leaf Litter ○ Mulch ○ Dead Tree or Wood ○ Grass
○ Soil ○ Other _____

Type of Tree(s) On or Near: _____

Forest Type: ○ Deciduous ○ Coniferous ○ Tropical ○ Other _____

Weather Conditions: _____

General

Size (overall height): _____ Color: _____ Spore Color: _____

Texture: ○ Tough ○ Brittle ○ Leathery ○ Woody ○ Soft ○ Slimy
○ Spongy ○ Powdery ○ Waxy ○ Rubbery ○ Watery (Other) _____

Bruising When Touched? ○ Yes ○ No   Notes: _____

Structures: ○ Cup ○ Ring ○ Warts   _____

Cap Characteristics

Campanulate
(bell-shaped)

Conical
(triangular)

Cylindrical
(shaped like half an egg)

Convex
(outwardly rounded)

Flat
(with top of
uniform height)

Infundibuliform
(deeply, depressed,
funnel-shaped)

Depressed
(with a low
central region)

Umbonate
(with a central
bump or knob)

Surface Markings (warts, scales, slime, etc.): _____

Cap Margin: Smooth, Inrolled, Sinuous/Wavy, Other: _____

Color Changes: _____

Undercap

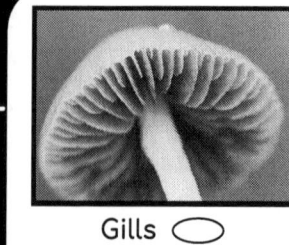

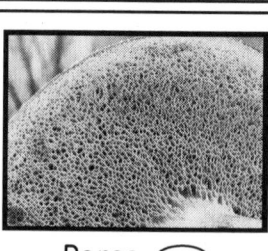

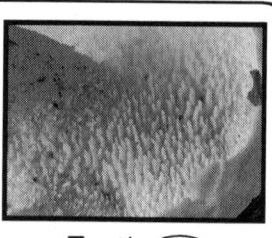

Gills ○

Attachment: Free or Decurrent

Spacing: Crowded, Close,
        Distant, Subdistant

Color/Bruising: _____

Pores ○

Color: _____

Pore Size: _____

Pore Pattern: _____

Teeth ○

Color: _____

Teeth Length: _____

Flesh: Soft or Tough

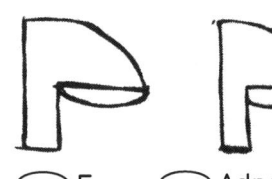

Free	Adnexed	Sinuate	Adnate	Descenting
(gills not attached to stem)	(gills attached narrowly to stem)	(gills smoothly notched and running briefly down stem)	(gills widely attached widely to stem)	(gills running down stem for some length)

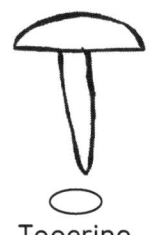

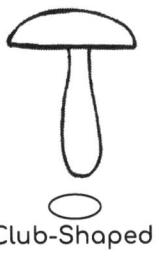
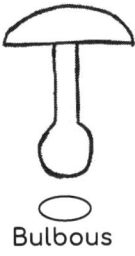
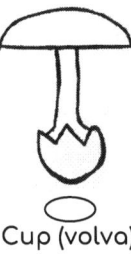

Tapering	Equal	Club-Shaped	Bulbous	Cup (volva)

Morels
- Edible ☺
- Honeycombed cap
- Most morels cap is longer than stem
- Spore print is usually light colored
- Interior is hollow

Puffballs
- Edible ☺
- Color is white
- Rounded-shaped balls with or without spiny warts on top
- Can be mistaken for golf ball, baseball or even soccer ball

Fly Agaric
- Poisonous ☹
- Red-brown cap - irregularly lobed, like a brain
- Tube-like hollows
- Yellowish spore print
- Smooth with more wrinkles as it ages

Oyster Mushroom
- Edible ☺
- Grows on hardwood trees
- Gills descend to base
- Gills are not saw toothed or ruffled
- Spore deposit gray

Death Cap
- Poisonous ☹
- Flattened top
- White cap with brownish scales
- Gills are free and white, turning green as they mature

Jack O'Lantern
- Poisonous ☹
- Bright orange to yellowish
- Grows in clusters
- Cap convex
- Gills narrow
- Cream spore print

Lion's Mane
- Edible ☺
- Covered all over with long, spine-like hairs
- Club-shaped fruit bodies
- Common on hardwoods

Destroying Angel
- Poisonous ☹
- White stalk and gills
- White cap or white edge and yellowish, pinkish, or tan center
- Egg-shaped cap

Chicken of the Woods
- Edible ☺
- Fan-shaped and suede-like texture
- Fruitbody with yellow, round pores
- Brownish color

Chanterelle
- Edible ☺
- Shape looks like bell of a trumpet
- Bright yellow/orange
- Similar look to Jack o'Lantern

Deadly Galerina
- Poisonous ☹
- Brownish, sticky cap, yellowish to rusty gills, ring on stalk
- Edges are curved against gills
- Gills narrow, crowded

Witches' Butter
- Edible ☺
- Small, yellow, irregularly lobed, gelatinous masses
- Grows on dead deciduous wood, especially oaks

Spore Print

_____

_____

_____

_____

_____

_____

Location

Site / GPS: _____ Date: _____

◯ Living Tree ◯ Leaf Litter ◯ Mulch ◯ Dead Tree or Wood ◯ Grass
◯ Soil ◯ Other _____

Type of Tree(s) On or Near: _____

Forest Type: ◯ Deciduous ◯ Coniferous ◯ Tropical ◯ Other _____

Weather Conditions: _____

General

Size (overall height): _____ Color: _____ Spore Color: _____

Texture: ◯ Tough ◯ Brittle ◯ Leathery ◯ Woody ◯ Soft ◯ Slimy
◯ Spongy ◯ Powdery ◯ Waxy ◯ Rubbery ◯ Watery (Other) _____

Bruising When Touched? ◯ Yes ◯ No   Notes: _____

Structures: ◯ Cup ◯ Ring ◯ Warts   _____

Cap Characteristics

Campanulate
(bell-shaped)

Conical
(triangular)

Cylindrical
(shaped like half an egg)

Convex
(outwardly rounded)

Flat
(with top of
uniform height)

Infundibuliform
(deeply, depressed,
funnel-shaped)

Depressed
(with a low
central region)

Umbonate
(with a central
bump or knob)

Surface Markings (warts, scales, slime, etc.): _____

Cap Margin: Smooth, Inrolled, Sinuous/Wavy, Other:_____

Color Changes: _____

Undercap

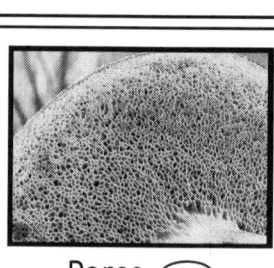

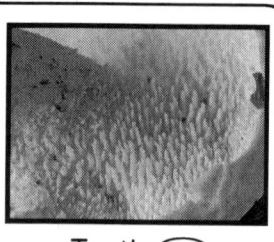

Gills ◯

Attachment: Free or Decurrent

Spacing: Crowded, Close,
Distant, Subdistant

Color/Bruising: _____

Pores ◯

Color: _____

Pore Size: _____

Pore Pattern: _____

Teeth ◯

Color: _____

Teeth Length: _____

Flesh: Soft or Tough

Free	Adnexed	Sinuate	Adnate	Descending
(gills not attached to stem)	(gills attached narrowly to stem)	(gills smoothly notched and running briefly down stem)	(gills widely attached widely to stem)	(gills running down stem for some length)

| Tapering | Equal | Club-Shaped | Bulbous | Cup (volva) |

Morels
- Edible ☺
- Honeycombed cap
- Most morels cap is longer than stem
- Spore print is usually light colored
- Interior is hollow

Puffballs
- Edible ☺
- Color is white
- Rounded-shaped balls with or without spiny warts on top
- Can be mistaken for golf ball, baseball or even soccer ball

Fly Agaric
- Poisonous ☹
- Red-brown cap - irregularly lobed, like a brain
- Tube-like hollows
- Yellowish spore print
- Smooth with more wrinkles as it ages

Oyster Mushroom
- Edible ☺
- Grows on hardwood trees
- Gills descend to base
- Gills are not saw toothed or ruffled
- Spore deposit gray

Death Cap
- Poisonous ☹
- Flattened top
- White cap with brownish scales
- Gills are free and white, turning green as they mature

Jack O'Lantern
- Poisonous ☹
- Bright orange to yellowish
- Grows in clusters
- Cap convex
- Gills narrow
- Cream spore print

Lion's Mane
- Edible ☺
- Covered all over with long, spine-like hairs
- Club-shaped fruit bodies
- Common on hardwoods

Destroying Angel
- Poisonous ☹
- White stalk and gills
- White cap or white edge and yellowish, pinkish, or tan center
- Egg-shaped cap

Chicken of the Woods
- Edible ☺
- Fan-shaped and suede-like texture
- Fruitbody with yellow, round pores
- Brownish color

Chanterelle
- Edible ☺
- Shape looks like bell of a trumpet
- Bright yellow/orange
- Similar look to Jack o'Lantern

Deadly Galerina
- Poisonous ☹
- Brownish, sticky cap, yellowish to rusty gills, ring on stalk
- Edges are curved against gills
- Gills narrow, crowded

Witches' Butter
- Edible ☺
- Small, yellow, irregularly lobed, gelatinous masses
- Grows on dead deciduous wood, especially oaks

Spore Print

_____

_____

_____

_____

_____

_____

Location

Site / GPS: _____ Date: _____

◯ Living Tree   ◯ Leaf Litter   ◯ Mulch   ◯ Dead Tree or Wood   ◯ Grass
◯ Soil   ◯ Other _____

Type of Tree(s) On or Near: _____

Forest Type: ◯ Deciduous   ◯ Coniferous   ◯ Tropical   ◯ Other _____

Weather Conditions: _____

General

Size (overall height): _____   Color: _____   Spore Color: _____

Texture: ◯ Tough ◯ Brittle ◯ Leathery ◯ Woody ◯ Soft ◯ Slimy
◯ Spongy ◯ Powdery ◯ Waxy ◯ Rubbery ◯ Watery (Other) _____

Bruising When Touched? ◯ Yes ◯ No   Notes: _____

Structures: ◯ Cup ◯ Ring ◯ Warts   _____

Cap Characteristics

Campanulate
(bell-shaped)

Conical
(triangular)

Cylindrical
(shaped like half an egg)

Convex
(outwardly rounded)

Flat
(with top of
uniform height)

Infundibuliform
(deeply, depressed,
funnel-shaped)

Depressed
(with a low
central region)

Umbonate
(with a central
bump or knob)

Surface Markings (warts, scales, slime, etc.): _____

Cap Margin: Smooth, Inrolled, Sinuous/Wavy, Other:_____

Color Changes: _____

Undercap

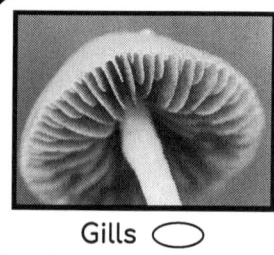

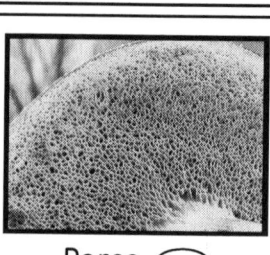
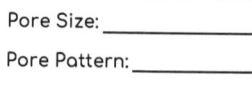

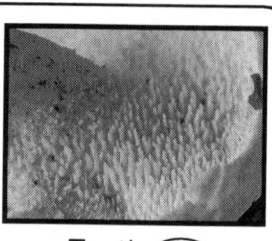

Gills ◯

Attachment: Free or Decurrent

Spacing: Crowded, Close,
        Distant, Subdistant

Color/Bruising: _____

Pores ◯

Color: _____

Pore Size: _____

Pore Pattern: _____

Teeth ◯

Color: _____

Teeth Length: _____

Flesh: Soft or Tough

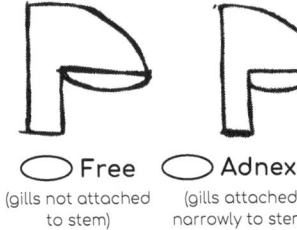

⬭ **Free**
(gills not attached to stem)

⬭ **Adnexed**
(gills attached narrowly to stem)

⬭ **Sinuate**
(gills smoothly notched and running briefly down stem)

⬭ **Adnate**
(gills widely attached widely to stem)

⬭ **Descending**
(gills running down stem for some length)

  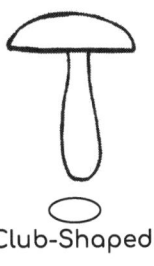 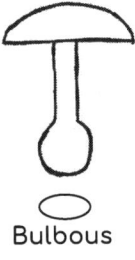 

⬭ **Tapering**   ⬭ **Equal**   ⬭ **Club-Shaped**   ⬭ **Bulbous**   ⬭ **Cup (volva)**

Morels

- Edible ☺
- Honeycombed cap
- Most morels cap is longer than stem
- Spore print is usually light colored
- Interior is hollow

Puffballs

- Edible ☺
- Color is white
- Rounded-shaped balls with or without spiny warts on top
- Can be mistaken for golf ball, baseball or even soccer ball

Fly Agaric

- Poisonous ☹
- Red-brown cap - irregularly lobed, like a brain
- Tube-like hollows
- Yellowish spore print
- Smooth with more wrinkles as it ages

Oyster Mushroom

- Edible ☺
- Grows on hardwood trees
- Gills descend to base
- Gills are not saw toothed or ruffled
- Spore deposit gray

Death Cap

- Poisonous ☹
- Flattened top
- White cap with brownish scales
- Gills are free and white, turning green as they mature

Jack O'Lantern

- Poisonous ☹
- Bright orange to yellowish
- Grows in clusters
- Cap convex
- Gills narrow
- Cream spore print

Lion's Mane

- Edible ☺
- Covered all over with long, spine-like hairs
- Club-shaped fruit bodies
- Common on hardwoods

Destroying Angel

- Poisonous ☹
- White stalk and gills
- White cap or white edge and yellowish, pinkish, or tan center
- Egg-shaped cap

Chicken of the Woods

- Edible ☺
- Fan-shaped and suede-like texture
- Fruitbody with yellow, round pores
- Brownish color

Chanterelle

- Edible ☺
- Shape looks like bell of a trumpet
- Bright yellow/orange
- Similar look to Jack o'Lantern

Deadly Galerina

- Poisonous ☹
- Brownish, sticky cap, yellowish to rusty gills, ring on stalk
- Edges are curved against gills
- Gills narrow, crowded

Witches' Butter

- Edible ☺
- Small, yellow, irregularly lobed, gelatinous masses
- Grows on dead deciduous wood, especially oaks

Spore Print

_____
_____
_____
_____
_____
_____

Location

Site / GPS: _____ Date: _____

◯ Living Tree   ◯ Leaf Litter   ◯ Mulch   ◯ Dead Tree or Wood   ◯ Grass
◯ Soil   ◯ Other _____

Type of Tree(s) On or Near: _____

Forest Type: ◯ Deciduous   ◯ Coniferous   ◯ Tropical   ◯ Other _____

Weather Conditions: _____

General

Size (overall height): _____   Color: _____   Spore Color: _____

Texture: ◯ Tough   ◯ Brittle   ◯ Leathery   ◯ Woody   ◯ Soft   ◯ Slimy
◯ Spongy   ◯ Powdery   ◯ Waxy   ◯ Rubbery   ◯ Watery   (Other) _____

Bruising When Touched? ◯ Yes   ◯ No   Notes: _____

Structures: ◯ Cup   ◯ Ring   ◯ Warts   _____

Cap Characteristics

Campanulate
(bell-shaped)

Conical
(triangular)

Cylindrical
(shaped like half an egg)

Convex
(outwardly rounded)

Flat
(with top of uniform height)

Infundibuliform
(deeply, depressed, funnel-shaped)

Depressed
(with a low central region)

Umbonate
(with a central bump or knob)

Surface Markings (warts, scales, slime, etc.): _____

Cap Margin: Smooth, Inrolled, Sinuous/Wavy, Other:_____

Color Changes: _____

Undercap

Gills ◯

Attachment: Free or Decurrent

Spacing: Crowded, Close, Distant, Subdistant

Color/Bruising: _____

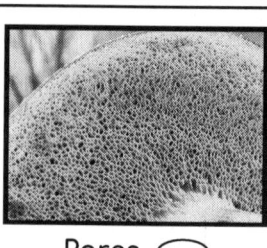

Pores ◯

Color: _____

Pore Size: _____

Pore Pattern: _____

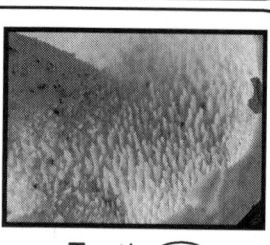

Teeth ◯

Color: _____

Teeth Length: _____

Flesh: Soft or Tough

◯ Free
(gills not attached to stem)

◯ Adnexed
(gills attached narrowly to stem)

◯ Sinuate
(gills smoothly notched and running briefly down stem)

◯ Adnate
(gills widely attached widely to stem)

◯ Descending
(gills running down stem for some length)

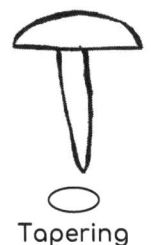  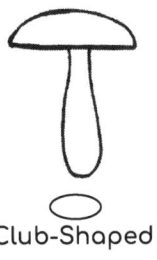 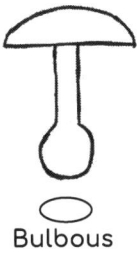 

◯ Tapering   ◯ Equal   ◯ Club-Shaped   ◯ Bulbous   ◯ Cup (volva)

Morels
- Edible ☺
- Honeycombed cap
- Most morels cap is longer than stem
- Spore print is usually light colored
- Interior is hollow

Puffballs
- Edible ☺
- Color is white
- Rounded-shaped balls with or without spiny warts on top
- Can be mistaken for golf ball, baseball or even soccer ball

Fly Agaric
- Poisonous ☹
- Red-brown cap - irregularly lobed, like a brain
- Tube-like hollows
- Yellowish spore print
- Smooth with more wrinkles as it ages

Oyster Mushroom
- Edible ☺
- Grows on hardwood trees
- Gills descend to base
- Gills are not saw toothed or ruffled
- Spore deposit gray

Death Cap
- Poisonous ☹
- Flattened top
- White cap with brownish scales
- Gills are free and white, turning green as they mature

Jack O'Lantern
- Poisonous ☹
- Bright orange to yellowish
- Grows in clusters
- Cap convex
- Gills narrow
- Cream spore print

Lion's Mane
- Edible ☺
- Covered all over with long, spine-like hairs
- Club-shaped fruit bodies
- Common on hardwoods

Destroying Angel
- Poisonous ☹
- White stalk and gills
- White cap or white edge and yellowish, pinkish, or tan center
- Egg-shaped cap

Chicken of the Woods
- Edible ☺
- Fan-shaped and suede-like texture
- Fruitbody with yellow, round pores
- Brownish color

Chanterelle
- Edible ☺
- Shape looks like bell of a trumpet
- Bright yellow/orange
- Similar look to Jack o'Lantern

Deadly Galerina
- Poisonous ☹
- Brownish, sticky cap, yellowish to rusty gills, ring on stalk
- Edges are curved against gills
- Gills narrow, crowded

Witches' Butter
- Edible ☺
- Small, yellow, irregularly lobed, gelatinous masses
- Grows on dead deciduous wood, especially oaks

Spore Print

_____
_____
_____
_____
_____
_____

Location

Site / GPS: _____ Date: _____

○ Living Tree ○ Leaf Litter ○ Mulch ○ Dead Tree or Wood ○ Grass
○ Soil ○ Other _____

Type of Tree(s) On or Near: _____

Forest Type: ○ Deciduous ○ Coniferous ○ Tropical ○ Other _____

Weather Conditions: _____

General

Size (overall height): _____ Color: _____ Spore Color: _____

Texture: ○ Tough ○ Brittle ○ Leathery ○ Woody ○ Soft ○ Slimy
○ Spongy ○ Powdery ○ Waxy ○ Rubbery ○ Watery (Other) _____

Bruising When Touched? ○ Yes ○ No   Notes: _____

Structures: ○ Cup ○ Ring ○ Warts   _____

Cap Characteristics

Campanulate
(bell-shaped)

Conical
(triangular)

Cylindrical
(shaped like half an egg)

Convex
(outwardly rounded)

Flat
(with top of
uniform height)

Infundibuliform
(deeply, depressed,
funnel-shaped)

Depressed
(with a low
central region)

Umbonate
(with a central
bump or knob)

Surface Markings (warts, scales, slime, etc.): _____

Cap Margin: Smooth, Inrolled, Sinuous/Wavy, Other: _____

Color Changes: _____

Undercap

Gills ○
Attachment: Free or Decurrent
Spacing: Crowded, Close,
        Distant, Subdistant
Color/Bruising: _____

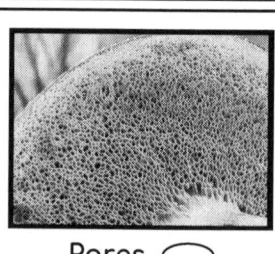

Pores ○
Color: _____
Pore Size: _____
Pore Pattern: _____

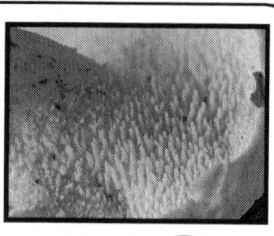

Teeth ○
Color: _____
Teeth Length: _____
Flesh: Soft or Tough

○ **Free**
(gills not attached to stem)

○ **Adnexed**
(gills attached narrowly to stem)

○ **Sinuate**
(gills smoothly notched and running briefly down stem)

○ **Adnate**
(gills widely attached widely to stem)

○ **Descending**
(gills running down stem for some length)

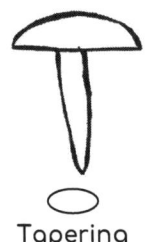 **Tapering**

 **Equal**

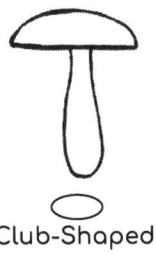 **Club-Shaped**

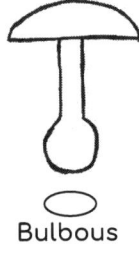 **Bulbous**

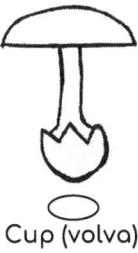 **Cup (volva)**

Morels
- Edible ☺
- Honeycombed cap
- Most morels cap is longer than stem
- Spore print is usually light colored
- Interior is hollow

Puffballs
- Edible ☺
- Color is white
- Rounded-shaped balls with or without spiny warts on top
- Can be mistaken for golf ball, baseball or even soccer ball

Fly Agaric
- Poisonous ☹
- Red-brown cap - irregularly lobed, like a brain
- Tube-like hollows
- Yellowish spore print
- Smooth with more wrinkles as it ages

Oyster Mushroom
- Edible ☺
- Grows on hardwood trees
- Gills descend to base
- Gills are not saw toothed or ruffled
- Spore deposit gray

Death Cap
- Poisonous ☹
- Flattened top
- White cap with brownish scales
- Gills are free and white, turning green as they mature

Jack O'Lantern
- Poisonous ☹
- Bright orange to yellowish
- Grows in clusters
- Cap convex
- Gills narrow
- Cream spore print

Lion's Mane
- Edible ☺
- Covered all over with long, spine-like hairs
- Club-shaped fruit bodies
- Common on hardwoods

Destroying Angel
- Poisonous ☹
- White stalk and gills
- White cap or white edge and yellowish, pinkish, or tan center
- Egg-shaped cap

Chicken of the Woods
- Edible ☺
- Fan-shaped and suede-like texture
- Fruitbody with yellow, round pores
- Brownish color

Chanterelle
- Edible ☺
- Shape looks like bell of a trumpet
- Bright yellow/orange
- Similar look to Jack o'Lantern

Deadly Galerina
- Poisonous ☹
- Brownish, sticky cap, yellowish to rusty gills, ring on stalk
- Edges are curved against gills
- Gills narrow, crowded

Witches' Butter
- Edible ☺
- Small, yellow, irregularly lobed, gelatinous masses
- Grows on dead deciduous wood, especially oaks

Spore Print

_____

_____

_____

_____

_____

_____

Location

Site / GPS: _____ Date: _____

◯ Living Tree ◯ Leaf Litter ◯ Mulch ◯ Dead Tree or Wood ◯ Grass
◯ Soil ◯ Other _____

Type of Tree(s) On or Near: _____

Forest Type: ◯ Deciduous ◯ Coniferous ◯ Tropical ◯ Other _____

Weather Conditions: _____

General

Size (overall height): _____ Color: _____ Spore Color: _____

Texture: ◯ Tough ◯ Brittle ◯ Leathery ◯ Woody ◯ Soft ◯ Slimy
◯ Spongy ◯ Powdery ◯ Waxy ◯ Rubbery ◯ Watery (Other) _____

Bruising When Touched? ◯ Yes ◯ No   Notes: _____

Structures: ◯ Cup ◯ Ring ◯ Warts   _____

Cap Characteristics

Campanulate
(bell-shaped)

Conical
(triangular)

Cylindrical
(shaped like half an egg)

Convex
(outwardly rounded)

Flat
(with top of
uniform height)

Infundibuliform
(deeply, depressed,
funnel-shaped)

Depressed
(with a low
central region)

Umbonate
(with a central
bump or knob)

Surface Markings (warts, scales, slime, etc.): _____

Cap Margin: Smooth, Inrolled, Sinuous/Wavy, Other: _____

Color Changes: _____

Undercap

Gills ◯
Attachment: Free or Decurrent
Spacing: Crowded, Close,
        Distant, Subdistant
Color/Bruising: _____

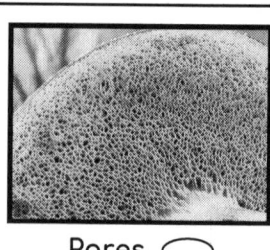
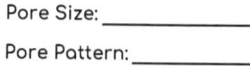

Pores ◯
Color: _____
Pore Size: _____
Pore Pattern: _____

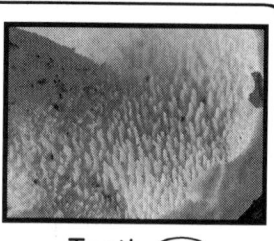

Teeth ◯
Color: _____
Teeth Length: _____
Flesh: Soft or Tough

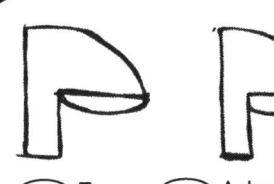

○ Free
(gills not attached to stem)

○ Adnexed
(gills attached narrowly to stem)

○ Sinuate
(gills smoothly notched and running briefly down stem)

○ Adnate
(gills widely attached widely to stem)

○ Descending
(gills running down stem for some length)

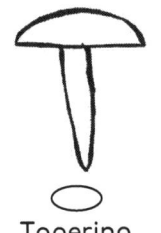

○ Tapering

○ Equal

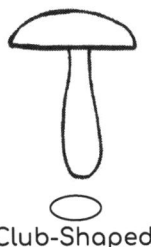

○ Club-Shaped

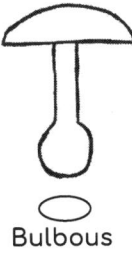

○ Bulbous

○ Cup (volva)

Morels
- Edible ☺
- Honeycombed cap
- Most morels cap is longer than stem
- Spore print is usually light colored
- Interior is hollow

Puffballs
- Edible ☺
- Color is white
- Rounded-shaped balls with or without spiny warts on top
- Can be mistaken for golf ball, baseball or even soccer ball

Fly Agaric
- Poisonous ☹
- Red-brown cap - irregularly lobed, like a brain
- Tube-like hollows
- Yellowish spore print
- Smooth with more wrinkles as it ages

Oyster Mushroom
- Edible ☺
- Grows on hardwood trees
- Gills descend to base
- Gills are not saw toothed or ruffled
- Spore deposit gray

Death Cap
- Poisonous ☹
- Flattened top
- White cap with brownish scales
- Gills are free and white, turning green as they mature

Jack O'Lantern
- Poisonous ☹
- Bright orange to yellowish
- Grows in clusters
- Cap convex
- Gills narrow
- Cream spore print

Lion's Mane
- Edible ☺
- Covered all over with long, spine-like hairs
- Club-shaped fruit bodies
- Common on hardwoods

Destroying Angel
- Poisonous ☹
- White stalk and gills
- White cap or white edge and yellowish, pinkish, or tan center
- Egg-shaped cap

Chicken of the Woods
- Edible ☺
- Fan-shaped and suede-like texture
- Fruitbody with yellow, round pores
- Brownish color

Chanterelle
- Edible ☺
- Shape looks like bell of a trumpet
- Bright yellow/orange
- Similar look to Jack o'Lantern

Deadly Galerina
- Poisonous ☹
- Brownish, sticky cap, yellowish to rusty gills, ring on stalk
- Edges are curved against gills
- Gills narrow, crowded

Witches' Butter
- Edible ☺
- Small, yellow, irregularly lobed, gelatinous masses
- Grows on dead deciduous wood, especially oaks

Spore Print

_____

_____

_____

_____

_____

_____

Location

Site / GPS: _____ Date: _____

○ Living Tree ○ Leaf Litter ○ Mulch ○ Dead Tree or Wood ○ Grass
○ Soil ○ Other _____

Type of Tree(s) On or Near: _____

Forest Type: ○ Deciduous ○ Coniferous ○ Tropical ○ Other _____

Weather Conditions: _____

General

Size (overall height): _____ Color: _____ Spore Color: _____

Texture: ○ Tough ○ Brittle ○ Leathery ○ Woody ○ Soft ○ Slimy
○ Spongy ○ Powdery ○ Waxy ○ Rubbery ○ Watery (Other) _____

Bruising When Touched? ○ Yes ○ No   Notes: _____

Structures: ○ Cup ○ Ring ○ Warts   _____

Cap Characteristics

Campanulate
(bell-shaped)

Conical
(triangular)

Cylindrical
(shaped like half an egg)

Convex
(outwardly rounded)

Flat
(with top of
uniform height)

Infundibuliform
(deeply, depressed,
funnel-shaped)

Depressed
(with a low
central region)

Umbonate
(with a central
bump or knob)

Surface Markings (warts, scales, slime, etc.): _____

Cap Margin: Smooth, Inrolled, Sinuous/Wavy, Other: _____

Color Changes: _____

Undercap

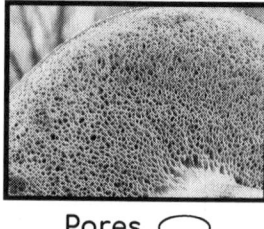

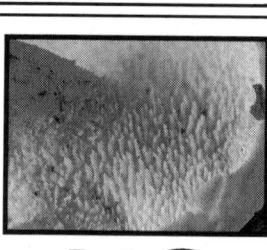

Gills ○

Attachment: Free or Decurrent

Spacing: Crowded, Close,
Distant, Subdistant

Color/Bruising: _____

Pores ○

Color: _____

Pore Size: _____

Pore Pattern: _____

Teeth ○

Color: _____

Teeth Length: _____

Flesh: Soft or Tough

◯ Free
(gills not attached to stem)

◯ Adnexed
(gills attached narrowly to stem)

◯ Sinuate
(gills smoothly notched and running briefly down stem)

◯ Adnate
(gills widely attached widely to stem)

◯ Descending
(gills running down stem for some length)

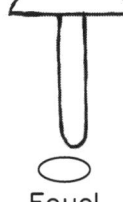
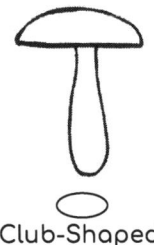
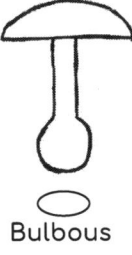

◯ Tapering
◯ Equal
◯ Club-Shaped
◯ Bulbous
◯ Cup (volva)

Morels

- Edible ☺
- Honeycombed cap
- Most morels cap is longer than stem
- Spore print is usually light colored
- Interior is hollow

Puffballs

- Edible ☺
- Color is white
- Rounded-shaped balls with or without spiny warts on top
- Can be mistaken for golf ball, baseball or even soccer ball

Fly Agaric

- Poisonous ☹
- Red-brown cap - irregularly lobed, like a brain
- Tube-like hollows
- Yellowish spore print
- Smooth with more wrinkles as it ages

Oyster Mushroom

- Edible ☺
- Grows on hardwood trees
- Gills descend to base
- Gills are not saw toothed or ruffled
- Spore deposit gray

Death Cap

- Poisonous ☹
- Flattened top
- White cap with brownish scales
- Gills are free and white, turning green as they mature

Jack O'Lantern

- Poisonous ☹
- Bright orange to yellowish
- Grows in clusters
- Cap convex
- Gills narrow
- Cream spore print

Lion's Mane

- Edible ☺
- Covered all over with long, spine-like hairs
- Club-shaped fruit bodies
- Common on hardwoods

Destroying Angel

- Poisonous ☹
- White stalk and gills
- White cap or white edge and yellowish, pinkish, or tan center
- Egg-shaped cap

Chicken of the Woods

- Edible ☺
- Fan-shaped and suede-like texture
- Fruitbody with yellow, round pores
- Brownish color

Chanterelle

- Edible ☺
- Shape looks like bell of a trumpet
- Bright yellow/orange
- Similar look to Jack o'Lantern

Deadly Galerina

- Poisonous ☹
- Brownish, sticky cap, yellowish to rusty gills, ring on stalk
- Edges are curved against gills
- Gills narrow, crowded

Witches' Butter

- Edible ☺
- Small, yellow, irregularly lobed, gelatinous masses
- Grows on dead deciduous wood, especially oaks

Spore Print

_____
_____
_____
_____
_____
_____

Location

Site / GPS: _____ Date: _____

◯ Living Tree ◯ Leaf Litter ◯ Mulch ◯ Dead Tree or Wood ◯ Grass
◯ Soil ◯ Other _____

Type of Tree(s) On or Near: _____

Forest Type: ◯ Deciduous ◯ Coniferous ◯ Tropical ◯ Other _____

Weather Conditions: _____

General

Size (overall height): _____ Color: _____ Spore Color: _____

Texture: ◯ Tough ◯ Brittle ◯ Leathery ◯ Woody ◯ Soft ◯ Slimy
◯ Spongy ◯ Powdery ◯ Waxy ◯ Rubbery ◯ Watery (Other) _____

Bruising When Touched? ◯ Yes ◯ No   Notes: _____

Structures: ◯ Cup ◯ Ring ◯ Warts   _____

Cap Characteristics

Campanulate
(bell-shaped)

Conical
(triangular)

Cylindrical
(shaped like half an egg)

Convex
(outwardly rounded)

Flat
(with top of
uniform height)

Infundibuliform
(deeply, depressed,
funnel-shaped)

Depressed
(with a low
central region)

Umbonate
(with a central
bump or knob)

Surface Markings (warts, scales, slime, etc.): _____

Cap Margin: Smooth, Inrolled, Sinuous/Wavy, Other: _____

Color Changes: _____

Undercap

Gills ◯

Attachment: Free or Decurrent

Spacing: Crowded, Close,
Distant, Subdistant

Color/Bruising: _____

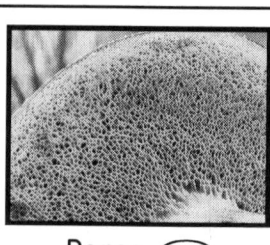

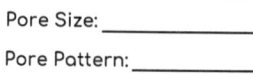

Pores ◯

Color: _____

Pore Size: _____

Pore Pattern: _____

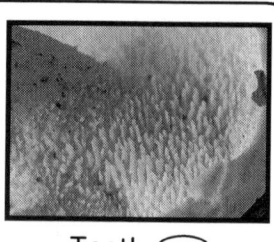

Teeth ◯

Color: _____

Teeth Length: _____

Flesh: Soft or Tough

○ Free
(gills not attached to stem)

○ Adnexed
(gills attached narrowly to stem)

○ Sinuate
(gills smoothly notched and running briefly down stem)

○ Adnate
(gills widely attached widely to stem)

○ Descenting
(gills running down stem for some length)

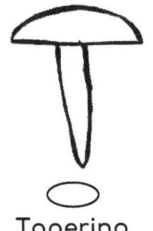  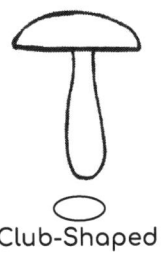 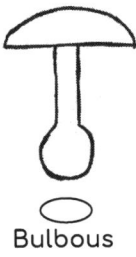 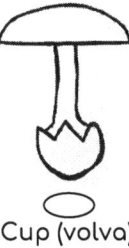 

Tapering
Equal
Club-Shaped
Bulbous
Cup (volva)

Morels
- Edible ☺
- Honeycombed cap
- Most morels cap is longer than stem
- Spore print is usually light colored
- Interior is hollow

Puffballs
- Edible ☺
- Color is white
- Rounded-shaped balls with or without spiny warts on top
- Can be mistaken for golf ball, baseball or even soccer ball

Fly Agaric
- Poisonous ☹
- Red-brown cap - irregularly lobed, like a brain
- Tube-like hollows
- Yellowish spore print
- Smooth with more wrinkles as it ages

Oyster Mushroom
- Edible ☺
- Grows on hardwood trees
- Gills descend to base
- Gills are not saw toothed or ruffled
- Spore deposit gray

Death Cap
- Poisonous ☹
- Flattened top
- White cap with brownish scales
- Gills are free and white, turning green as they mature

Jack O'Lantern
- Poisonous ☹
- Bright orange to yellowish
- Grows in clusters
- Cap convex
- Gills narrow
- Cream spore print

Lion's Mane
- Edible ☺
- Covered all over with long, spine-like hairs
- Club-shaped fruit bodies
- Common on hardwoods

Destroying Angel
- Poisonous ☹
- White stalk and gills
- White cap or white edge and yellowish, pinkish, or tan center
- Egg-shaped cap

Chicken of the Woods
- Edible ☺
- Fan-shaped and suede-like texture
- Fruitbody with yellow, round pores
- Brownish color

Chanterelle
- Edible ☺
- Shape looks like bell of a trumpet
- Bright yellow/orange
- Similar look to Jack o'Lantern

Deadly Galerina
- Poisonous ☹
- Brownish, sticky cap, yellowish to rusty gills, ring on stalk
- Edges are curved against gills
- Gills narrow, crowded

Witches' Butter
- Edible ☺
- Small, yellow, irregularly lobed, gelatinous masses
- Grows on dead deciduous wood, especially oaks

Spore Print

_____

_____

_____

_____

_____

_____

Location

Site / GPS: _____ Date: _____

○ Living Tree ○ Leaf Litter ○ Mulch ○ Dead Tree or Wood ○ Grass
○ Soil ○ Other _____

Type of Tree(s) On or Near: _____

Forest Type: ○ Deciduous ○ Coniferous ○ Tropical ○ Other _____

Weather Conditions: _____

General

Size (overall height): _____ Color: _____ Spore Color: _____

Texture: ○ Tough ○ Brittle ○ Leathery ○ Woody ○ Soft ○ Slimy
○ Spongy ○ Powdery ○ Waxy ○ Rubbery ○ Watery (Other) _____

Bruising When Touched? ○ Yes ○ No   Notes: _____

Structures: ○ Cup ○ Ring ○ Warts   _____

Cap Characteristics

Campanulate
(bell-shaped)

Conical
(triangular)

Cylindrical
(shaped like half an egg)

Convex
(outwardly rounded)

Flat
(with top of
uniform height)

Infundibuliform
(deeply, depressed,
funnel-shaped)

Depressed
(with a low
central region)

Umbonate
(with a central
bump or knob)

Surface Markings (warts, scales, slime, etc.): _____

Cap Margin: Smooth, Inrolled, Sinuous/Wavy, Other: _____

Color Changes: _____

Undercap

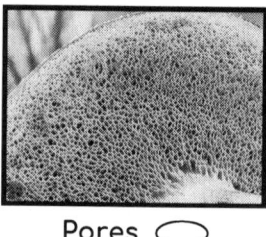

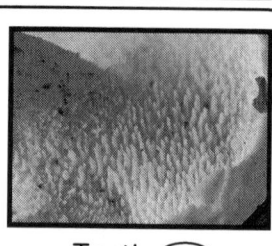

Gills ○

Attachment: Free or Decurrent

Spacing: Crowded, Close,
Distant, Subdistant

Color/Bruising: _____

Pores ○

Color: _____

Pore Size: _____

Pore Pattern: _____

Teeth ○

Color: _____

Teeth Length: _____

Flesh: Soft or Tough

○ Free
(gills not attached to stem)

○ Adnexed
(gills attached narrowly to stem)

○ Sinuate
(gills smoothly notched and running briefly down stem)

○ Adnate
(gills widely attached widely to stem)

○ Descenting
(gills running down stem for some length)

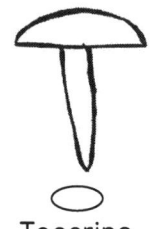  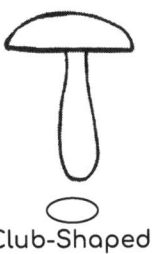 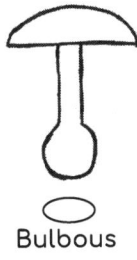  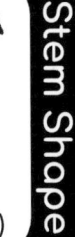

Tapering   Equal   Club-Shaped   Bulbous   Cup (volva)

Morels
- Edible ☺
- Honeycombed cap
- Most morels cap is longer than stem
- Spore print is usually light colored
- Interior is hollow

Puffballs
- Edible ☺
- Color is white
- Rounded-shaped balls with or without spiny warts on top
- Can be mistaken for golf ball, baseball or even soccer ball

Fly Agaric
- Poisonous ☹
- Red-brown cap - irregularly lobed, like a brain
- Tube-like hollows
- Yellowish spore print
- Smooth with more wrinkles as it ages

Oyster Mushroom
- Edible ☺
- Grows on hardwood trees
- Gills descend to base
- Gills are not saw toothed or ruffled
- Spore deposit gray

Death Cap
- Poisonous ☹
- Flattened top
- White cap with brownish scales
- Gills are free and white, turning green as they mature

Jack O'Lantern
- Poisonous ☹
- Bright orange to yellowish
- Grows in clusters
- Cap convex
- Gills narrow
- Cream spore print

Lion's Mane
- Edible ☺
- Covered all over with long, spine-like hairs
- Club-shaped fruit bodies
- Common on hardwoods

Destroying Angel
- Poisonous ☹
- White stalk and gills
- White cap or white edge and yellowish, pinkish, or tan center
- Egg-shaped cap

Chicken of the Woods
- Edible ☺
- Fan-shaped and suede-like texture
- Fruitbody with yellow, round pores
- Brownish color

Chanterelle
- Edible ☺
- Shape looks like bell of a trumpet
- Bright yellow/orange
- Similar look to Jack o'Lantern

Deadly Galerina
- Poisonous ☹
- Brownish, sticky cap, yellowish to rusty gills, ring on stalk
- Edges are curved against gills
- Gills narrow, crowded

Witches' Butter
- Edible ☺
- Small, yellow, irregularly lobed, gelatinous masses
- Grows on dead deciduous wood, especially oaks

Spore Print

_____

_____

_____

_____

_____

Location

Site / GPS: _____ Date: _____

○ Living Tree ○ Leaf Litter ○ Mulch ○ Dead Tree or Wood ○ Grass
○ Soil ○ Other _____

Type of Tree(s) On or Near: _____

Forest Type: ○ Deciduous ○ Coniferous ○ Tropical ○ Other _____

Weather Conditions: _____

General

Size (overall height): _____ Color: _____ Spore Color: _____

Texture: ○ Tough ○ Brittle ○ Leathery ○ Woody ○ Soft ○ Slimy
○ Spongy ○ Powdery ○ Waxy ○ Rubbery ○ Watery (Other) _____

Bruising When Touched? ○ Yes ○ No   Notes: _____

Structures: ○ Cup ○ Ring ○ Warts   _____

Cap Characteristics

Campanulate
(bell-shaped)

Conical
(triangular)

Cylindrical
(shaped like half an egg)

Convex
(outwardly rounded)

Flat
(with top of
uniform height)

Infundibuliform
(deeply, depressed,
funnel-shaped)

Depressed
(with a low
central region)

Umbonate
(with a central
bump or knob)

Surface Markings (warts, scales, slime, etc.): _____

Cap Margin: Smooth, Inrolled, Sinuous/Wavy, Other: _____

Color Changes: _____

Undercap

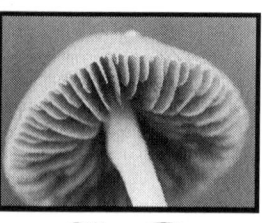

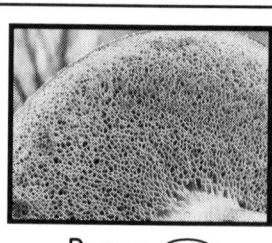

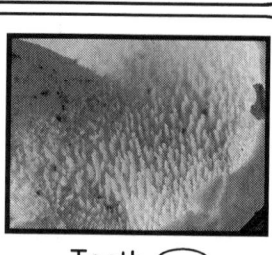

Gills ○

Attachment: Free or Decurrent

Spacing: Crowded, Close,
Distant, Subdistant

Color/Bruising: _____

Pores ○

Color: _____

Pore Size: _____

Pore Pattern: _____

Teeth ○

Color: _____

Teeth Length: _____

Flesh: Soft or Tough

- Free
(gills not attached to stem)
- Adnexed
(gills attached narrowly to stem)
- Sinuate
(gills smoothly notched and running briefly down stem)
- Adnate
(gills widely attached widely to stem)
- Descending
(gills running down stem for some length)

- Tapering
- Equal
- Club-Shaped
- Bulbous
- Cup (volva)

Morels
- Edible ☺
- Honeycombed cap
- Most morels cap is longer than stem
- Spore print is usually light colored
- Interior is hollow

Puffballs
- Edible ☺
- Color is white
- Rounded-shaped balls with or without spiny warts on top
- Can be mistaken for golf ball, baseball or even soccer ball

Fly Agaric
- Poisonous ☻
- Red-brown cap - irregularly lobed, like a brain
- Tube-like hollows
- Yellowish spore print
- Smooth with more wrinkles as it ages

Oyster Mushroom
- Edible ☺
- Grows on hardwood trees
- Gills descend to base
- Gills are not saw toothed or ruffled
- Spore deposit gray

Death Cap
- Poisonous ☻
- Flattened top
- White cap with brownish scales
- Gills are free and white, turning green as they mature

Jack O'Lantern
- Poisonous ☻
- Bright orange to yellowish
- Grows in clusters
- Cap convex
- Gills narrow
- Cream spore print

Lion's Mane
- Edible ☺
- Covered all over with long, spine-like hairs
- Club-shaped fruit bodies
- Common on hardwoods

Destroying Angel
- Poisonous ☻
- White stalk and gills
- White cap or white edge and yellowish, pinkish, or tan center
- Egg-shaped cap

Chicken of the Woods
- Edible ☺
- Fan-shaped and suede-like texture
- Fruitbody with yellow, round pores
- Brownish color

Chanterelle
- Edible ☺
- Shape looks like bell of a trumpet
- Bright yellow/orange
- Similar look to Jack o'Lantern

Deadly Galerina
- Poisonous ☻
- Brownish, sticky cap, yellowish to rusty gills, ring on stalk
- Edges are curved against gills
- Gills narrow, crowded

Witches' Butter
- Edible ☺
- Small, yellow, irregularly lobed, gelatinous masses
- Grows on dead deciduous wood, especially oaks

Spore Print

_____
_____
_____
_____
_____

Location

Site / GPS: _____ Date: _____

○ Living Tree ○ Leaf Litter ○ Mulch ○ Dead Tree or Wood ○ Grass
○ Soil ○ Other _____

Type of Tree(s) On or Near: _____

Forest Type: ○ Deciduous ○ Coniferous ○ Tropical ○ Other _____

Weather Conditions: _____

General

Size (overall height): _____ Color: _____ Spore Color: _____

Texture: ○ Tough ○ Brittle ○ Leathery ○ Woody ○ Soft ○ Slimy
○ Spongy ○ Powdery ○ Waxy ○ Rubbery ○ Watery (Other) _____

Bruising When Touched? ○ Yes ○ No   Notes: _____

Structures: ○ Cup ○ Ring ○ Warts   _____

Cap Characteristics

Campanulate
(bell-shaped)

Conical
(triangular)

Cylindrical
(shaped like half an egg)

Convex
(outwardly rounded)

Flat
(with top of
uniform height)

Infundibuliform
(deeply, depressed,
funnel-shaped)

Depressed
(with a low
central region)

Umbonate
(with a central
bump or knob)

Surface Markings (warts, scales, slime, etc.): _____

Cap Margin: Smooth, Inrolled, Sinuous/Wavy, Other: _____

Color Changes: _____

Undercap

Gills ○

Attachment: Free or Decurrent

Spacing: Crowded, Close,
Distant, Subdistant

Color/Bruising: _____

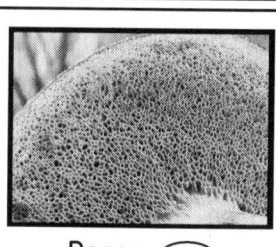

Pores ○

Color: _____

Pore Size: _____

Pore Pattern: _____

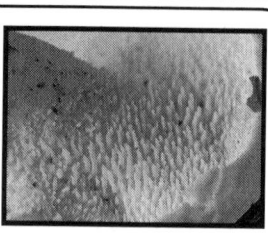

Teeth ○

Color: _____

Teeth Length: _____

Flesh: Soft or Tough

○ Free
(gills not attached to stem)

○ Adnexed
(gills attached narrowly to stem)

○ Sinuate
(gills smoothly notched and running briefly down stem)

○ Adnate
(gills widely attached widely to stem)

○ Descending
(gills running down stem for some length)

  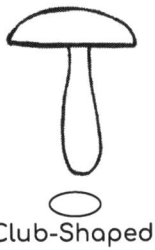 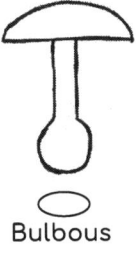 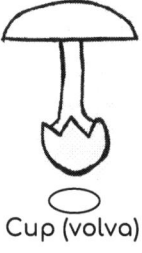

Tapering | Equal | Club-Shaped | Bulbous | Cup (volva)

Morels
- Edible ☺
- Honeycombed cap
- Most morels cap is longer than stem
- Spore print is usually light colored
- Interior is hollow

Puffballs
- Edible ☺
- Color is white
- Rounded-shaped balls with or without spiny warts on top
- Can be mistaken for golf ball, baseball or even soccer ball

Fly Agaric
- Poisonous ☹
- Red-brown cap - irregularly lobed, like a brain
- Tube-like hollows
- Yellowish spore print
- Smooth with more wrinkles as it ages

Oyster Mushroom
- Edible ☺
- Grows on hardwood trees
- Gills descend to base
- Gills are not saw toothed or ruffled
- Spore deposit gray

Death Cap
- Poisonous ☹
- Flattened top
- White cap with brownish scales
- Gills are free and white, turning green as they mature

Jack O'Lantern
- Poisonous ☹
- Bright orange to yellowish
- Grows in clusters
- Cap convex
- Gills narrow
- Cream spore print

Lion's Mane
- Edible ☺
- Covered all over with long, spine-like hairs
- Club-shaped fruit bodies
- Common on hardwoods

Destroying Angel
- Poisonous ☹
- White stalk and gills
- White cap or white edge and yellowish, pinkish, or tan center
- Egg-shaped cap

Chicken of the Woods
- Edible ☺
- Fan-shaped and suede-like texture
- Fruitbody with yellow, round pores
- Brownish color

Chanterelle
- Edible ☺
- Shape looks like bell of a trumpet
- Bright yellow/orange
- Similar look to Jack o'Lantern

Deadly Galerina
- Poisonous ☹
- Brownish, sticky cap, yellowish to rusty gills, ring on stalk
- Edges are curved against gills
- Gills narrow, crowded

Witches' Butter
- Edible ☺
- Small, yellow, irregularly lobed, gelatinous masses
- Grows on dead deciduous wood, especially oaks

Spore Print

_____

_____

_____

_____

_____

_____

Location

Site / GPS: _____ Date: _____

⃝ Living Tree ⃝ Leaf Litter ⃝ Mulch ⃝ Dead Tree or Wood ⃝ Grass
⃝ Soil ⃝ Other _____

Type of Tree(s) On or Near: _____

Forest Type: ⃝ Deciduous ⃝ Coniferous ⃝ Tropical ⃝ Other _____

Weather Conditions: _____

General

Size (overall height): _____ Color: _____ Spore Color: _____

Texture: ⃝ Tough ⃝ Brittle ⃝ Leathery ⃝ Woody ⃝ Soft ⃝ Slimy
⃝ Spongy ⃝ Powdery ⃝ Waxy ⃝ Rubbery ⃝ Watery (Other) _____

Bruising When Touched? ⃝ Yes ⃝ No   Notes: _____

Structures: ⃝ Cup ⃝ Ring ⃝ Warts   _____

Cap Characteristics

Campanulate
(bell-shaped)

Conical
(triangular)

Cylindrical
(shaped like half an egg)

Convex
(outwardly rounded)

Flat
(with top of
uniform height)

Infundibuliform
(deeply, depressed,
funnel-shaped)

Depressed
(with a low
central region)

Umbonate
(with a central
bump or knob)

Surface Markings (warts, scales, slime, etc.): _____

Cap Margin: Smooth, Inrolled, Sinuous/Wavy, Other: _____

Color Changes: _____

Undercap

Gills ⃝

Attachment: Free or Decurrent

Spacing: Crowded, Close,
Distant, Subdistant

Color/Bruising: _____

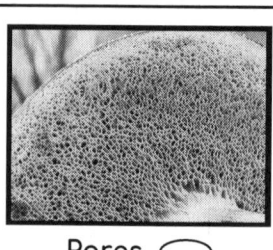

Pores ⃝

Color: _____

Pore Size: _____

Pore Pattern: _____

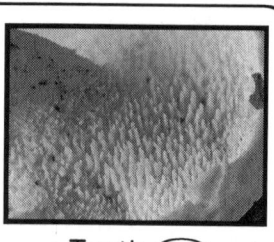

Teeth ⃝

Color: _____

Teeth Length: _____

Flesh: Soft or Tough

○ Free
(gills not attached to stem)

○ Adnexed
(gills attached narrowly to stem)

○ Sinuate
(gills smoothly notched and running briefly down stem)

○ Adnate
(gills widely attached widely to stem)

○ Descenting
(gills running down stem for some length)

  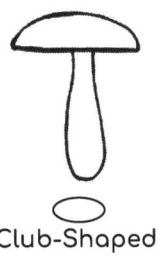 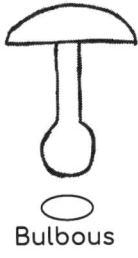 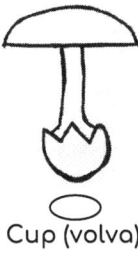

○ Tapering   ○ Equal   ○ Club-Shaped   ○ Bulbous   ○ Cup (volva)

Morels
- Edible ☺
- Honeycombed cap
- Most morels cap is longer than stem
- Spore print is usually light colored
- Interior is hollow

Puffballs
- Edible ☺
- Color is white
- Rounded-shaped balls with or without spiny warts on top
- Can be mistaken for golf ball, baseball or even soccer ball

Fly Agaric
- Poisonous ☹
- Red-brown cap - irregularly lobed, like a brain
- Tube-like hollows
- Yellowish spore print
- Smooth with more wrinkles as it ages

Oyster Mushroom
- Edible ☺
- Grows on hardwood trees
- Gills descend to base
- Gills are not saw toothed or ruffled
- Spore deposit gray

Death Cap
- Poisonous ☹
- Flattened top
- White cap with brownish scales
- Gills are free and white, turning green as they mature

Jack O'Lantern
- Poisonous ☹
- Bright orange to yellowish
- Grows in clusters
- Cap convex
- Gills narrow
- Cream spore print

Lion's Mane
- Edible ☺
- Covered all over with long, spine-like hairs
- Club-shaped fruit bodies
- Common on hardwoods

Destroying Angel
- Poisonous ☹
- White stalk and gills
- White cap or white edge and yellowish, pinkish, or tan center
- Egg-shaped cap

Chicken of the Woods
- Edible ☺
- Fan-shaped and suede-like texture
- Fruitbody with yellow, round pores
- Brownish color

Chanterelle
- Edible ☺
- Shape looks like bell of a trumpet
- Bright yellow/orange
- Similar look to Jack o'Lantern

Deadly Galerina
- Poisonous ☹
- Brownish, sticky cap, yellowish to rusty gills, ring on stalk
- Edges are curved against gills
- Gills narrow, crowded

Witches' Butter
- Edible ☺
- Small, yellow, irregularly lobed, gelatinous masses
- Grows on dead deciduous wood, especially oaks

Spore Print

_____

_____

_____

_____

_____

_____

Location

Site / GPS: _____ Date: _____

○ Living Tree   ○ Leaf Litter   ○ Mulch   ○ Dead Tree or Wood   ○ Grass
○ Soil   ○ Other _____

Type of Tree(s) On or Near: _____

Forest Type: ○ Deciduous   ○ Coniferous   ○ Tropical   ○ Other _____

Weather Conditions: _____

General

Size (overall height): _____   Color: _____   Spore Color: _____

Texture: ○ Tough   ○ Brittle   ○ Leathery   ○ Woody   ○ Soft   ○ Slimy
○ Spongy   ○ Powdery   ○ Waxy   ○ Rubbery   ○ Watery   (Other) _____

Bruising When Touched? ○ Yes   ○ No   Notes: _____

Structures: ○ Cup   ○ Ring   ○ Warts   _____

Cap Characteristics

Campanulate
(bell-shaped)

Conical
(triangular)

Cylindrical
(shaped like half an egg)

Convex
(outwardly rounded)

Flat
(with top of uniform height)

Infundibuliform
(deeply, depressed, funnel-shaped)

Depressed
(with a low central region)

Umbonate
(with a central bump or knob)

Surface Markings (warts, scales, slime, etc.): _____

Cap Margin: Smooth, Inrolled, Sinuous/Wavy, Other: _____

Color Changes: _____

Undercap

Gills ○

Attachment: Free or Decurrent

Spacing: Crowded, Close, Distant, Subdistant

Color/Bruising: _____

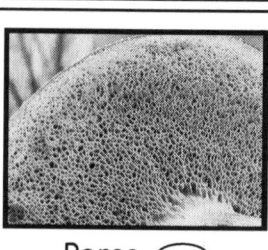

Pores ○

Color: _____

Pore Size: _____

Pore Pattern: _____

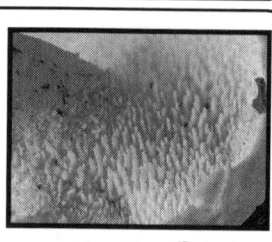

Teeth ○

Color: _____

Teeth Length: _____

Flesh: Soft or Tough

Free
(gills not attached to stem)

Adnexed
(gills attached narrowly to stem)

Sinuate
(gills smoothly notched and running briefly down stem)

 **Adnate**
(gills widely attached widely to stem)

 **Descending**
(gills running down stem for some length)

  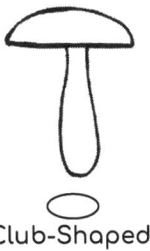 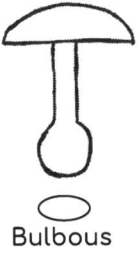 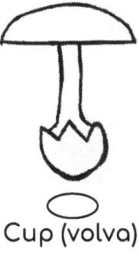

Tapering   **Equal**   **Club-Shaped**   **Bulbous**   **Cup (volva)**

Morels
- Edible ☺
- Honeycombed cap
- Most morels cap is longer than stem
- Spore print is usually light colored
- Interior is hollow

Puffballs
- Edible ☺
- Color is white
- Rounded-shaped balls with or without spiny warts on top
- Can be mistaken for golf ball, baseball or even soccer ball

Fly Agaric
- Poisonous ☹
- Red-brown cap - irregularly lobed, like a brain
- Tube-like hollows
- Yellowish spore print
- Smooth with more wrinkles as it ages

Oyster Mushroom
- Edible ☺
- Grows on hardwood trees
- Gills descend to base
- Gills are not saw toothed or ruffled
- Spore deposit gray

Death Cap
- Poisonous ☹
- Flattened top
- White cap with brownish scales
- Gills are free and white, turning green as they mature

Jack O'Lantern
- Poisonous ☹
- Bright orange to yellowish
- Grows in clusters
- Cap convex
- Gills narrow
- Cream spore print

Lion's Mane
- Edible ☺
- Covered all over with long, spine-like hairs
- Club-shaped fruit bodies
- Common on hardwoods

Destroying Angel
- Poisonous ☹
- White stalk and gills
- White cap or white edge and yellowish, pinkish, or tan center
- Egg-shaped cap

Chicken of the Woods
- Edible ☺
- Fan-shaped and suede-like texture
- Fruitbody with yellow, round pores
- Brownish color

Chanterelle
- Edible ☺
- Shape looks like bell of a trumpet
- Bright yellow/orange
- Similar look to Jack o'Lantern

Deadly Galerina
- Poisonous ☹
- Brownish, sticky cap, yellowish to rusty gills, ring on stalk
- Edges are curved against gills
- Gills narrow, crowded

Witches' Butter
- Edible ☺
- Small, yellow, irregularly lobed, gelatinous masses
- Grows on dead deciduous wood, especially oaks

Spore Print

Location

Site / GPS: _____ Date: _____

○ Living Tree ○ Leaf Litter ○ Mulch ○ Dead Tree or Wood ○ Grass
○ Soil ○ Other _____

Type of Tree(s) On or Near: _____

Forest Type: ○ Deciduous ○ Coniferous ○ Tropical ○ Other _____

Weather Conditions: _____

General

Size (overall height): _____ Color: _____ Spore Color: _____

Texture: ○ Tough ○ Brittle ○ Leathery ○ Woody ○ Soft ○ Slimy
○ Spongy ○ Powdery ○ Waxy ○ Rubbery ○ Watery (Other) _____

Bruising When Touched? ○ Yes ○ No Notes: _____

Structures: ○ Cup ○ Ring ○ Warts _____

Cap Characteristics

Campanulate
(bell-shaped)

Conical
(triangular)

Cylindrical
(shaped like half an egg)

Convex
(outwardly rounded)

Flat
(with top of
uniform height)

Infundibuliform
(deeply, depressed,
funnel-shaped)

Depressed
(with a low
central region)

Umbonate
(with a central
bump or knob)

Surface Markings (warts, scales, slime, etc.): _____

Cap Margin: Smooth, Inrolled, Sinuous/Wavy, Other: _____

Color Changes: _____

Undercap

Gills ○

Attachment: Free or Decurrent

Spacing: Crowded, Close,
        Distant, Subdistant

Color/Bruising: _____

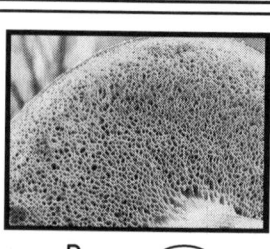

Pores ○

Color: _____

Pore Size: _____

Pore Pattern: _____

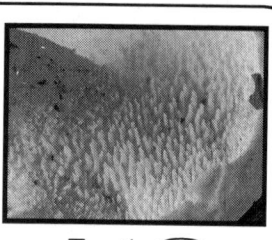

Teeth ○

Color: _____

Teeth Length: _____

Flesh: Soft or Tough

○ Free
(gills not attached to stem)

Adnexed
(gills attached narrowly to stem)

Sinuate
(gills smoothly notched and running briefly down stem)

Adnate
(gills widely attached widely to stem)

Descending
(gills running down stem for some length)

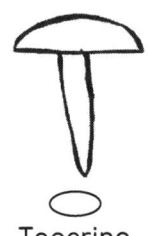  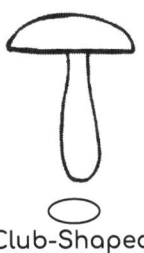 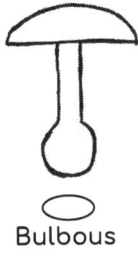 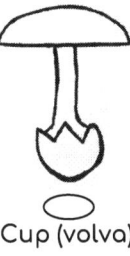

Tapering · Equal · Club-Shaped · Bulbous · Cup (volva)

Morels
- Edible ☺
- Honeycombed cap
- Most morels cap is longer than stem
- Spore print is usually light colored
- Interior is hollow

Puffballs
- Edible ☺
- Color is white
- Rounded-shaped balls with or without spiny warts on top
- Can be mistaken for golf ball, baseball or even soccer ball

Fly Agaric
- Poisonous ☹
- Red-brown cap - irregularly lobed, like a brain
- Tube-like hollows
- Yellowish spore print
- Smooth with more wrinkles as it ages

Oyster Mushroom
- Edible ☺
- Grows on hardwood trees
- Gills descend to base
- Gills are not saw toothed or ruffled
- Spore deposit gray

Death Cap
- Poisonous ☹
- Flattened top
- White cap with brownish scales
- Gills are free and white, turning green as they mature

Jack O'Lantern
- Poisonous ☹
- Bright orange to yellowish
- Grows in clusters
- Cap convex
- Gills narrow
- Cream spore print

Lion's Mane
- Edible ☺
- Covered all over with long, spine-like hairs
- Club-shaped fruit bodies
- Common on hardwoods

Destroying Angel
- Poisonous ☹
- White stalk and gills
- White cap or white edge and yellowish, pinkish, or tan center
- Egg-shaped cap

Chicken of the Woods
- Edible ☺
- Fan-shaped and suede-like texture
- Fruitbody with yellow, round pores
- Brownish color

Chanterelle
- Edible ☺
- Shape looks like bell of a trumpet
- Bright yellow/orange
- Similar look to Jack o'Lantern

Deadly Galerina
- Poisonous ☹
- Brownish, sticky cap, yellowish to rusty gills, ring on stalk
- Edges are curved against gills
- Gills narrow, crowded

Witches' Butter
- Edible ☺
- Small, yellow, irregularly lobed, gelatinous masses
- Grows on dead deciduous wood, especially oaks

Notes

Spore Print

_____
_____
_____
_____
_____
_____

Location

Site / GPS: _____ Date: _____

◯ Living Tree ◯ Leaf Litter ◯ Mulch ◯ Dead Tree or Wood ◯ Grass
◯ Soil ◯ Other _____

Type of Tree(s) On or Near: _____

Forest Type: ◯ Deciduous ◯ Coniferous ◯ Tropical ◯ Other _____

Weather Conditions: _____

General

Size (overall height): _____ Color: _____ Spore Color: _____

Texture: ◯ Tough ◯ Brittle ◯ Leathery ◯ Woody ◯ Soft ◯ Slimy
◯ Spongy ◯ Powdery ◯ Waxy ◯ Rubbery ◯ Watery (Other) _____

Bruising When Touched? ◯ Yes ◯ No Notes: _____

Structures: ◯ Cup ◯ Ring ◯ Warts _____

Cap Characteristics

Campanulate
(bell-shaped)

Conical
(triangular)

Cylindrical
(shaped like half an egg)

Convex
(outwardly rounded)

Flat
(with top of
uniform height)

Infundibuliform
(deeply, depressed,
funnel-shaped)

Depressed
(with a low
central region)

Umbonate
(with a central
bump or knob)

Surface Markings (warts, scales, slime, etc.): _____

Cap Margin: Smooth, Inrolled, Sinuous/Wavy, Other: _____

Color Changes: _____

Undercap

Gills ◯

Attachment: Free or Decurrent

Spacing: Crowded, Close,
Distant, Subdistant

Color/Bruising: _____

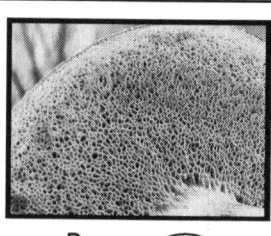

Pores ◯

Color: _____

Pore Size: _____

Pore Pattern: _____

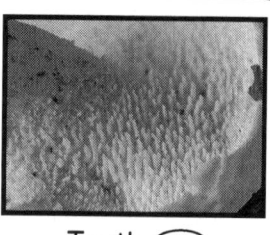

Teeth ◯

Color: _____

Teeth Length: _____

Flesh: Soft or Tough

Gill Attachment

- ⭕ **Free**
  (gills not attached to stem)
- ⭕ **Adnexed**
  (gills attached narrowly to stem)
- ⭕ **Sinuate**
  (gills smoothly notched and running briefly down stem)
- ⭕ **Adnate**
  (gills widely attached widely to stem)
- ⭕ **Descending**
  (gills running down stem for some length)

Stem Shape

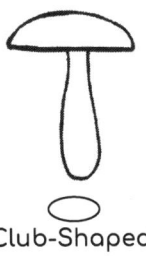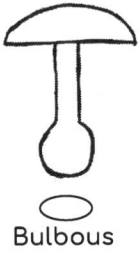

- ⭕ **Tapering**
- ⭕ **Equal**
- ⭕ **Club-Shaped**
- ⭕ **Bulbous**
- ⭕ **Cup (volva)**

Common Mushrooms

Morels
- Edible ☺
- Honeycombed cap
- Most morels cap is longer than stem
- Spore print is usually light colored
- Interior is hollow

Puffballs
- Edible ☺
- Color is white
- Rounded-shaped balls with or without spiny warts on top
- Can be mistaken for golf ball, baseball or even soccer ball

Fly Agaric
- Poisonous ☹
- Red-brown cap - irregularly lobed, like a brain
- Tube-like hollows
- Yellowish spore print
- Smooth with more wrinkles as it ages

Oyster Mushroom
- Edible ☺
- Grows on hardwood trees
- Gills descend to base
- Gills are not saw toothed or ruffled
- Spore deposit gray

Death Cap
- Poisonous ☹
- Flattened top
- White cap with brownish scales
- Gills are free and white, turning green as they mature

Jack O'Lantern
- Poisonous ☹
- Bright orange to yellowish
- Grows in clusters
- Cap convex
- Gills narrow
- Cream spore print

Lion's Mane
- Edible ☺
- Covered all over with long, spine-like hairs
- Club-shaped fruit bodies
- Common on hardwoods

Destroying Angel
- Poisonous ☹
- White stalk and gills
- White cap or white edge and yellowish, pinkish, or tan center
- Egg-shaped cap

Chicken of the Woods
- Edible ☺
- Fan-shaped and suede-like texture
- Fruitbody with yellow, round pores
- Brownish color

Chanterelle
- Edible ☺
- Shape looks like bell of a trumpet
- Bright yellow/orange
- Similar look to Jack o'Lantern

Deadly Galerina
- Poisonous ☹
- Brownish, sticky cap, yellowish to rusty gills, ring on stalk
- Edges are curved against gills
- Gills narrow, crowded

Witches' Butter
- Edible ☺
- Small, yellow, irregularly lobed, gelatinous masses
- Grows on dead deciduous wood, especially oaks

Notes

Spore Print

_____
_____
_____
_____
_____
_____

Location

Site / GPS: _____ Date: _____

○ Living Tree   ○ Leaf Litter   ○ Mulch   ○ Dead Tree or Wood   ○ Grass
○ Soil   ○ Other _____

Type of Tree(s) On or Near: _____

Forest Type: ○ Deciduous   ○ Coniferous   ○ Tropical   ○ Other _____

Weather Conditions: _____

General

Size (overall height): _____   Color: _____   Spore Color: _____

Texture: ○ Tough ○ Brittle ○ Leathery ○ Woody ○ Soft ○ Slimy
○ Spongy ○ Powdery ○ Waxy ○ Rubbery ○ Watery (Other) _____

Bruising When Touched? ○ Yes ○ No   Notes: _____

Structures: ○ Cup ○ Ring ○ Warts   _____

Cap Characteristics

Campanulate
(bell-shaped)

Conical
(triangular)

Cylindrical
(shaped like half an egg)

Convex
(outwardly rounded)

Flat
(with top of
uniform height)

Infundibuliform
(deeply, depressed,
funnel-shaped)

Depressed
(with a low
central region)

Umbonate
(with a central
bump or knob)

Surface Markings (warts, scales, slime, etc.): _____

Cap Margin: Smooth, Inrolled, Sinuous/Wavy, Other: _____

Color Changes: _____

Undercap

Gills ○

Attachment: Free or Decurrent

Spacing: Crowded, Close,
           Distant, Subdistant

Color/Bruising: _____

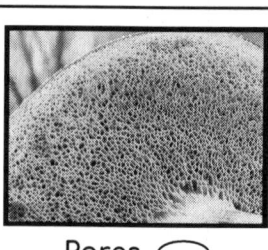

Pores ○

Color: _____

Pore Size: _____

Pore Pattern: _____

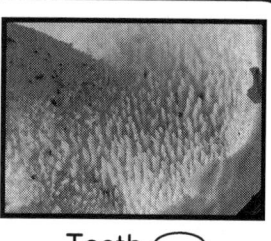

Teeth ○

Color: _____

Teeth Length: _____

Flesh: Soft or Tough

Gill Attachment

Free
(gills not attached to stem)

Adnexed
(gills attached narrowly to stem)

Sinuate
(gills smoothly notched and running briefly down stem)

Adnate
(gills widely attached widely to stem)

Descenting
(gills running down stem for some length)

Stem Shape

  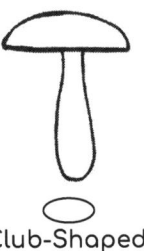 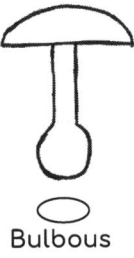 

Tapering

Equal

Club-Shaped

Bulbous

Cup (volva)

Common Mushrooms

Morels
- Edible ☺
- Honeycombed cap
- Most morels cap is longer than stem
- Spore print is usually light colored
- Interior is hollow

Puffballs
- Edible ☺
- Color is white
- Rounded-shaped balls with or without spiny warts on top
- Can be mistaken for golf ball, baseball or even soccer ball

Fly Agaric
- Poisonous ☹
- Red-brown cap - irregularly lobed, like a brain
- Tube-like hollows
- Yellowish spore print
- Smooth with more wrinkles as it ages

Oyster Mushroom
- Edible ☺
- Grows on hardwood trees
- Gills descend to base
- Gills are not saw toothed or ruffled
- Spore deposit gray

Death Cap
- Poisonous ☹
- Flattened top
- White cap with brownish scales
- Gills are free and white, turning green as they mature

Jack O'Lantern
- Poisonous ☹
- Bright orange to yellowish
- Grows in clusters
- Cap convex
- Gills narrow
- Cream spore print

Lion's Mane
- Edible ☺
- Covered all over with long, spine-like hairs
- Club-shaped fruit bodies
- Common on hardwoods

Destroying Angel
- Poisonous ☹
- White stalk and gills
- White cap or white edge and yellowish, pinkish, or tan center
- Egg-shaped cap

Chicken of the Woods
- Edible ☺
- Fan-shaped and suede-like texture
- Fruitbody with yellow, round pores
- Brownish color

Chanterelle
- Edible ☺
- Shape looks like bell of a trumpet
- Bright yellow/orange
- Similar look to Jack o'Lantern

Deadly Galerina
- Poisonous ☹
- Brownish, sticky cap, yellowish to rusty gills, ring on stalk
- Edges are curved against gills
- Gills narrow, crowded

Witches' Butter
- Edible ☺
- Small, yellow, irregularly lobed, gelatinous masses
- Grows on dead deciduous wood, especially oaks

Notes

Spore Print

_____

_____

_____

_____

_____

_____

Location

Site / GPS: _____ Date: _____

◯ Living Tree ◯ Leaf Litter ◯ Mulch ◯ Dead Tree or Wood ◯ Grass
◯ Soil ◯ Other _____

Type of Tree(s) On or Near: _____

Forest Type: ◯ Deciduous ◯ Coniferous ◯ Tropical ◯ Other _____

Weather Conditions: _____

General

Size (overall height): _____ Color: _____ Spore Color: _____

Texture: ◯ Tough ◯ Brittle ◯ Leathery ◯ Woody ◯ Soft ◯ Slimy
◯ Spongy ◯ Powdery ◯ Waxy ◯ Rubbery ◯ Watery (Other) _____

Bruising When Touched? ◯ Yes ◯ No Notes: _____

Structures: ◯ Cup ◯ Ring ◯ Warts   _____

Cap Characteristics

Campanulate
(bell-shaped)

Conical
(triangular)

Cylindrical
(shaped like half an egg)

Convex
(outwardly rounded)

Flat
(with top of uniform height)

Infundibuliform
(deeply, depressed, funnel-shaped)

Depressed
(with a low central region)

Umbonate
(with a central bump or knob)

Surface Markings (warts, scales, slime, etc.): _____

Cap Margin: Smooth, Inrolled, Sinuous/Wavy, Other: _____

Color Changes: _____

Undercap

Gills ◯
Attachment: Free or Decurrent

Spacing: Crowded, Close, Distant, Subdistant

Color/Bruising: _____

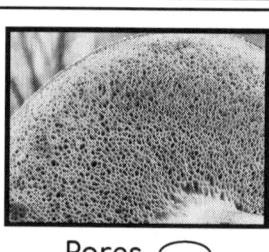

Pores ◯
Color: _____

Pore Size: _____

Pore Pattern: _____

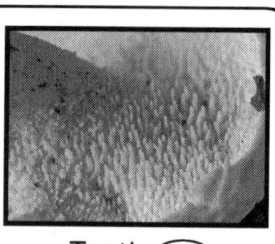

Teeth ◯
Color: _____

Teeth Length: _____

Flesh: Soft or Tough

Free
(gills not attached to stem)

Adnexed
(gills attached narrowly to stem)

Sinuate
(gills smoothly notched and running briefly down stem)

Adnate
(gills widely attached widely to stem)

Descending
(gills running down stem for some length)

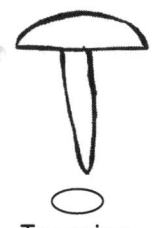

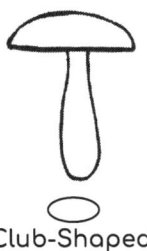
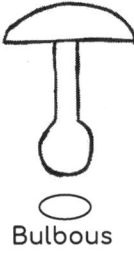

Tapering   **Equal**   **Club-Shaped**   **Bulbous**   **Cup (volva)**

Morels
- Edible ☺
- Honeycombed cap
- Most morels cap is longer than stem
- Spore print is usually light colored
- Interior is hollow

Puffballs
- Edible ☺
- Color is white
- Rounded-shaped balls with or without spiny warts on top
- Can be mistaken for golf ball, baseball or even soccer ball

Fly Agaric
- Poisonous ☹
- Red-brown cap - irregularly lobed, like a brain
- Tube-like hollows
- Yellowish spore print
- Smooth with more wrinkles as it ages

Oyster Mushroom
- Edible ☺
- Grows on hardwood trees
- Gills descend to base
- Gills are not saw toothed or ruffled
- Spore deposit gray

Death Cap
- Poisonous ☹
- Flattened top
- White cap with brownish scales
- Gills are free and white, turning green as they mature

Jack O'Lantern
- Poisonous ☹
- Bright orange to yellowish
- Grows in clusters
- Cap convex
- Gills narrow
- Cream spore print

Lion's Mane
- Edible ☺
- Covered all over with long, spine-like hairs
- Club-shaped fruit bodies
- Common on hardwoods

Destroying Angel
- Poisonous ☹
- White stalk and gills
- White cap or white edge and yellowish, pinkish, or tan center
- Egg-shaped cap

Chicken of the Woods
- Edible ☺
- Fan-shaped and suede-like texture
- Fruitbody with yellow, round pores
- Brownish color

Chanterelle
- Edible ☺
- Shape looks like bell of a trumpet
- Bright yellow/orange
- Similar look to Jack o'Lantern

Deadly Galerina
- Poisonous ☹
- Brownish, sticky cap, yellowish to rusty gills, ring on stalk
- Edges are curved against gills
- Gills narrow, crowded

Witches' Butter
- Edible ☺
- Small, yellow, irregularly lobed, gelatinous masses
- Grows on dead deciduous wood, especially oaks

Spore Print

_____

_____

_____

_____

_____

_____

Made in the USA
Columbia, SC
21 July 2022

63817337R00065